Fort Baker Through the Years
The Post, the Park, the Lodge

By Kristin L. Baron and John A. Martini

Hole in the Head Press
Bodega Bay, California

For information on reprinting and purchasing, contact:

Hole in the Head Press
Samuel E. Stokes, Publisher
P.O. Box 807, Bodega Bay, CA 94923
sestokes@sonic.net
www.holeintheheadpress.com

1 2 3 4 5 6 7 8 9

ISBN: 978-0-9761494-2-2

Library of Congress Control Number: 2011928309

Publisher: Samuel E. Stokes
Design and production: Carole Thickstun
Maps: Lawrence Ormsby
Editor: Susan Tasaki
Index: Bookmark: Editing & Indexing

The publisher gratefully acknowledges the generosity of the
Golden Gate National Recreation Area Park Archives,
which provided many of the photos that appear in this book.

For a full list of photo credits, see p. 95

Printed and bound in Canada

Table of Contents

Introduction
The Post, the Park, the Future

Bordered by San Francisco Bay on the south, the Marin hills on the west and north, and the promontory of Point Cavallo on the east, the former military post of Fort Baker is a natural refuge. This sheltered, bowl-shaped valley and its gentle waterfront have drawn people here for thousands of years.

Over the centuries, this land has seen many things: family bands of local Coast Miwok people; a sprawling Mexican-era cattle rancho; camouflaged army fortifications, barracks and cozy military residences; a Coast Guard lighthouse and rescue station; and, today, National Park Service personnel and Cavallo Point: The Lodge at the Golden Gate. The one thing it has never seen? Battle.

California's coastal mountains extend hundreds of miles north and south of San Francisco, separating the Pacific Ocean from the state's vast Central Valley. In that entire distance—approximately 800 miles—there is only one opening between ocean and interior: the Golden Gate, fabled portal into San Francisco Bay. Through this gap flow the waters from the half-dozen river systems that drain the state's interior from as far away as the Sierra Nevada. On flood tide, the brisk currents of the Pacific Ocean race eastward through the Gate into the bay, often moving at 4.5 to 7.5 knots, more than twice the flow of the Mississippi River. Thick banks of fog build up offshore during the summer months and are drawn inland, spreading over the bay and the densely packed cities that crowd its perimeter.

Fort Baker is located hard by the Golden Gate, only a few hundred yards from the iconic, mile-wide strait, yet sheltered from its harsher elements by the Marin Headlands. The fort's grassy parade ground and quaint military residences are often bathed in sunshine when the rest of the Bay Area is enduring blasts of cold ocean air and the impenetrable fogs that sometimes obscure the fort's most famous tenant, the Golden Gate Bridge.

The fort was originally designed as the northern hinge post of a pair of US Army forts that would keep enemy fleets from entering San Francisco Bay through the Golden Gate. First envisioned during the Gold Rush and continuing through the Cold War era, several generations of military defenses were sited here. Though Fort Baker was continuously garrisoned, the generations of soldiers who stood guard here for more than a century never fired a shot in anger. Fort Baker, and the rest of the Bay Area's forts, waited for enemies that never came. But by their very presence, they presented a deterrent force to would-be aggressors—the Spanish fleet of 1898, prowling World War II Japanese submarines or Soviet "Bear" bombers of the Cold War—who might have considered attacking San Francisco.

As the twenty-first century approached, the army moved out of the Marin Headlands and transferred Fort Baker and the rest of its former real estate holdings to the National Park Service, the nation's preservation agency, whose mission was to maintain the fort's historic buildings and surrounding open space "for the enjoyment of future generations." To help accomplish this goal, the park service began searching for appropriate tenants for the aging buildings that dotted the grounds, tenants who would serve as partners in giving new life to this historic army post.

At Fort Baker, partnership and preservation reached a dramatic and happy pinnacle with the 2008 opening of Cavallo Point, the Lodge at the Golden Gate, a landmark example of historic preservation.

Read on to discover the complete story of Fort Baker—from post to park and beyond.

XII

dess. et Lith. par Choris.

Lith. de Langlumé.

Coiffures de danse des habitans de la Californie.

Chapter One
The First Residents

It isn't hard to understand why people have always been drawn to this quiet valley and Horseshoe Cove, its sheltered waterfront. Long before Europeans knew of the existence of San Francisco Bay, the hills and coves lining the north shore near its entrance were the lands of the Huimen people, one of several Coast Miwok tribes who lived in the area now referred to as Marin County. Their villages dotted the Marin coast and bayshore from present-day Sausalito to southern Sonoma County.

The Huimen didn't live at Horseshoe Cove, at least not on a year-round basis, but rather, moved between permanent village sites and temporary hunting grounds at the bay's edge. The Huimen and other Coast Miwok lived according to a seasonal cycle, an annual rhythm that involved hunting, fishing and gathering. Periodically, they burned the land to promote the growth of native grasses for seed gathering and to create forage areas for deer, elk and other game.

The nearest Coast Miwok lived in a village named Livaneglua, two miles to the north in today's downtown Sausalito. They harvested acorns and medicinal shrubs in the valleys and hillsides surrounding the future Fort Baker, and hunted elk, deer and bear with obsidian-pointed arrows and spears. In tule-reed canoes, they plied the bay's waters, harvesting its abundance: waterfowl, sturgeon, shark, oysters and mussels, sea otters, and seals.

The Coast Miwok's world was an insular one. Although they were excellent sailors who regularly crossed the quiet parts of the bay, they didn't venture into rough water or beyond the harbor mouth. To them, the opening was an entrance to an unknown world where the sun disappeared and the dead went to rest. Later explorers would name it the Golden Gate.

The first European explorers to see San Francisco Bay came upon the harbor quite by accident. In October 1769, a group of Spanish soldiers searching for Monterey Bay overshot their mark and instead, found themselves looking from a coastal bluff onto a vast arm of the sea extending inland. The exploration party recognized immediately that this was not Monterey but instead, a previously unexplored bay of immense size and unknown resources. Other expeditions followed, and in August 1775, the first European ship entered the bay, a tiny packet boat named *San Carlos*, barely 80 feet long, commanded by Lt. Juan Manuel de Ayala.

The *San Carlos* anchored for several weeks in what is now Ayala Cove on Angel Island while the crew surveyed the harbor. According to Father Vicente de Santa Maria, chaplain of the *San Carlos* crew, the Huimen cautiously contacted the Spanish the day of their arrival, and the two groups and other local tribes exchanged visits and gifts, both aboard the ship and at the native people's villages.

Opposite: Historical images of Coast Miwoks are extremely rare, so for information, we rely on European artists who sketched and painted Native Americans they met on their journeys. In 1819, French artist Louis Choris visited San Francisco Bay and created this portrait of three native people dressed for a ceremonial dance. Choris did not record the people's tribal affiliation or homeland, but as they are native to the area, this art provides a visual complement to Fr. Santa Maria's description of the Coast Miwok he met near Cavallo Point.

From the journal of Father Vicente de Santa Maria aboard the *San Carlos*, San Francisco Bay, 1775

The local tribes had many opportunities to meet and interact with the Spanish during the explorers' six-week stay. In his journal for August 6, 1775, Father Vicente de Santa Maria, the ship's 37-year-old chaplain, recorded the Europeans' first encounter with the Huimen, which took place just north of Cavallo Point.

> Before the longboat had gone a quarter of a league it came across a *rancheria* [tribal village] . . . seeing that our people were close by, [the occupants] left their huts and stood scattered at the shore's edge. They were not dumbfounded (though naturally apprehensive at the sight of people strange to them); rather, one of them, raising his voice, began with much gesticulation to make a long speech in his language. . . . At the same time, they were making signs for the longboat to come near, giving assurance of peace by throwing their arrows to the ground and coming in front of them to show their innocence of deception or treachery.

The next day, Fr. Santa Maria went ashore to meet the Huimen.

> The Indians who came on this occasion were nine in number, three being old men, two of them with sight impaired by cataracts of some sort. The six others were young men of good presence and fine stature. . . . [T]he best favored were models of perfection. . . . One alone of the young men had several dark blue lines painted from the lower lip to the waist and from the left shoulder to the right, in such a way as to form a perfect cross. . . .

> Besides comely elegance of figure and quite faultless countenance, there was also—as their chief adornment—the way they did up their long hair; after smoothing it well they stuck in it a four-toothed wooden comb and bound up the ends in a net of cord and very small feathers that were dyed a deep red; and in the middle of the coiffure was tied a sort of ribbon, sometimes black, sometimes blue. . . .

> It would have seemed natural that these Indians, in their astonishment at our clothes, should have expressed a particular surprise, and no less curiosity; but they gave no sign of it. . . . We noticed an unusual thing about the young men: none of them ventured to speak and only their elders replied to us.

Late afternoon on August 5, 1775. The Spanish paquebot
San Carlos *prepared to sail through the Golden Gate strait.
For safety, Captain Ayala ordered the water depth measured
with a lead line as his ship entered unknown bay, unaware
the entrance was more than 300 feet deep.*

How Cavallo Point Got Its Name

When choosing a place name, Spanish and Mexican residents of Alta California frequently labeled them in honor of Catholic saints or religious themes, such as *San Francisco de Asis* for Saint Francis of Assisi and *Nuestra Señora de las Mercedes* for Our Lady of Mercy. In some cases, place names were simply descriptions of landscape features: *Saucelito* for the "Place of the Small Willows" or *Punta Boneta* for a point of land shaped like a hat.

When he applied for his land grant in 1838, William Richardson prepared a map of the proposed Rancho Saucelito that included an area labeled *Plaza de los Caballos*, or Horse Place, probably because of horses pastured on its slopes. Over the years, American mispronunciation of the original Spanish name *caballo* resulted in today's name for the Fort Baker area: Cavallo Point.

During their stay, the Spanish gave place names to many geographic features, though only a few of these names have survived. Among them, *Isla de los Alcatraces* (Island of the Sea Birds) for Alcatraz Island and *Isla de Nuestra Senora de los Angeles* (Island of Our Lady of the Angels) for Angel Island. To the dramatic harbor entrance, Lt. Juan Manuel de Ayala gave the prosaic but accurate title, *la Boca del Puerto* (the harbor mouth).

As the *San Carlos* tried to sail out through the harbor's mouth to return to Mexico, strong headwinds smashed it onto the rocks at what is today Lime Point. This was a mishap with which any modern-day sailor could sympathize; the tides and winds at the Golden Gate are among the coast's most treacherous. The ship spent ten days anchored in Horseshoe Cove while her crew made repairs to the rudder.

As a result of their collision with the rocky point, Ayala gave Fort Baker its first recorded name: *Punta de San Carlos*, in honor of their damaged ship. In later years, Americans named this finger of rocks "Lime Point" for the bird guano—heavy with white lime—that thickly coated the rocks and made them appear to be whitewashed.

A year later, in March 1776, a much larger land expedition that included both soldiers and civilian settlers arrived to establish a mission and an army post (or *presidio*) on the shores of San Francisco Bay. The mission of the Spanish army was to make sure the rest of the world's navies—especially the British and Russian fleets—were kept out of the magnificent bay of San Francisco and to protect the expansive harbor for Spain's use alone. This was the end of Spain's imperial colonization of North America, and San Francisco was the most far-flung outpost of the empire.

Unlike other areas in which they settled, the Spanish did not establish a civilian *pueblo* (community) when they arrived. Aside from a handful of dependents living near the Presidio of San Francisco and at the missions that sprang up around the bay, there were virtually no European civilian settlements here during the Spanish years.

All of the lands colonized by the Spanish in what was then known as *Alta* (or upper) California were seized from the native people by the authority of the military. Under the Spanish, the missions controlled the land while the army provided security. Private land ownership in California was almost unknown, and only a handful of royal land grants were given out to individuals in recognition of service to the Spanish crown.

Part of Spain's policy was to move indigenous tribes from their traditional homelands to the missions, where they would be Christianized and taught various trades. Spanish soldiers and Franciscan missionaries relocated entire villages to the new mission of *San Francisco de Asis* (also called Mission Dolores), where the native people lived in barracks-like conditions and learned agricultural and construction skills. In 1783, several members of the Huimen community were among the first Coast Miwoks to leave their homelands in Marin and move to Mission Dolores.

Their reasons for going to the missions were complex. In

many cases, the local peoples' worlds were in tumult, the result of food shortages, increasing infant-mortality rates and breakdowns in the older tribal systems. It was a time of few choices. The Spanish and their missions were often perceived as a new authority, and people were sometimes willing to enter the missions because they thought life would be better there. But once inside, they all too often faced poor hygienic conditions, crowded living quarters and rigid discipline. They were also exposed to new diseases against which they had no immunity, and for which no adequate treatments existed, either traditional or European.

The Franciscans realized that living conditions and the cold, damp climate at Mission Dolores were unhealthy, and in 1817, opened a new mission at San Raphael in Marin to serve both as a sort of hospital annex to San Francisco and to expand their proselytizing efforts farther north. The new mission's land holding extended all the way to the harbor entrance and included the former lands of the Huimen tribe and the future location of Fort Baker.

There is little in the historical record about what uses, if any, the Spanish had for the lands once occupied by Coast Miwok at the southern tip of Marin. Cowhands from Mission San Raphael used much of this area as grazing land for the mission's cattle, but it's not known if the herds roamed as far south as the Marin Headlands and Horseshoe Cove.

After Mexico seceded from Spain in 1822, the mission system lost much of its power. Consequently, mission lands, although directed by law to remain in the possession of Coast Miwoks and other native tribes, began being granted to Mexican citizens instead. This land-grant practice increased significantly after 1833, when an act of the Mexican legislature secularized the missions and took away their remaining land holdings. The former mission lands were broken up into vast private ranchos, some encompassing tens of thousands of acres, and cattle ranching became the primary industry.

Many of Alta California's European and American residents, in order to qualify for land, became naturalized Mexican citizens. In 1838, the Mexican government granted the southernmost portion of the Marin peninsula to William Antonio Richardson, a British-born Mexican citizen who had immigrated there several years before. Richardson's rancho was an impressive piece of real estate, encompassing 19,000 acres that stretched from the southern flank of Mount Tamalpais to the Pacific Ocean and San Francisco Bay. Richardson named his sprawling land grant *Rancho Saucelito* (Ranch of the Small Willows) and built a home near the former Coast Miwok village site of Livaneglua. Like most rancho owners, Richardson used his coastal hillsides primarily for grazing herds of cattle that he raised for their hides and fat.

For the next ten years, Rancho Saucelito and the other Mexican land grants around the bay carried out a lucrative trade with American trading ships. These so-called Boston Ships made the months-long voyage around Cape Horn and arrived in San Francisco Bay laden with all manner of manufactured items needed (or desired) in Mexican California: shoes, bolts of cloth, furniture, musical instruments, farming implements. The rancho owners traded with the Yankee ship owners, offering tanned cow hides and tubs of tallow (animal fat) in return for the imported Yankee goods. This came to be known as the "hide-and-tallow trade."

As the hide-and-tallow trade expanded, American ships arrived annually and anchored in a shallow inlet called Yerba Buena Cove on the southern side of the harbor's entrance. Earlier, in 1835, Richardson had been appointed Captain of the Port and established a central trading post and customhouse on the shore of Yerba Buena, a tiny pueblo that would soon explode into the city of San Francisco.

The Coast Miwok Today

Although devastated by European diseases and appallingly high child mortality rates, the Coast Miwok people survived this tragic episode in their history. Descendants of the people who met the Spanish explorers in 1775 are today a federally recognized tribe: the Federated Indians of Graton Rancheria. The Tribal Council works closely with the National Park Service on projects within the park today, and provided the authors with important guidance in the preparation of this book.

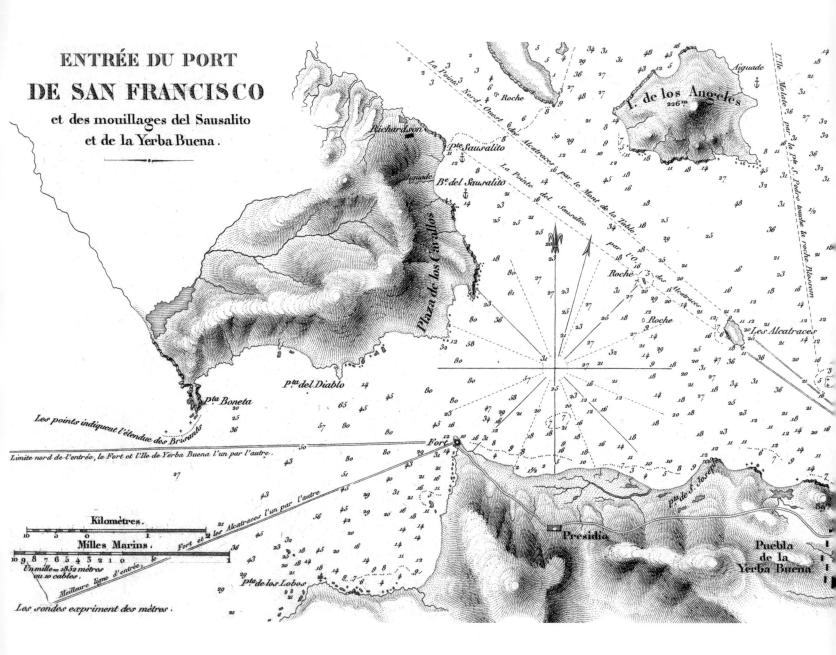

A French navigation chart from 1844 shows the undeveloped Marin Headlands and Plaza de los Cavallos, site of today's Fort Baker.

Chapter Two
The United States and Lime Point Military Reserve: 1850 to 1866

The hide-and-tallow trade, along with the entire rich *Californio* culture, would come to a dramatic end in early 1848, when two momentous events took place within days of each other: the signing of the Treaty of Guadalupe Hidalgo on February 2, 1848, which ended the Mexican-American War and ceded Alta California and much of the Southwest to the United States, and the discovery of gold in the Sierra Nevada foothills nine days previous.

As news of gold strikes made its way around the world, San Francisco's population skyrocketed from around 500 people in 1848 to nearly 35,000 in 1850. A vibrant but essentially lawless city sprang up along the shores of old Yerba Buena Cove. More than 500 ships were anchored in the bay, most of them abandoned by their gold-seeking crews. Soon, shipyards, factories, banks, an arsenal and even a branch of the US Mint were established to support the new metropolis. Tens of millions of dollars in gold were being shipped through the Golden Gate annually.

During the Gold Rush, San Francisco was a long way from the rest of the United States. No roads or railroads crossed the continent yet, and telegraph communication was a decade away. The fastest connection with the East Coast took many weeks and required crossing the disease-ridden Isthmus of Panama. San Francisco and its harbor of gold were literally undefended. If attacked, help would be a long time coming.

The US Army was charged with defending America's valu-

able new prize from foreign fleets, especially the British and the Russians, who had also established permanent outposts on the Pacific Coast.

Many years earlier, in 1794, the Spanish army had half-heartedly defended the harbor entrance by constructing a small adobe fort on the south side of the strait. Their tiny *Castillo* [castle] *de San Joaquin*, located on the site of today's Fort Point, had at one time mounted thirteen guns, but the Mexican military force that had succeeded the Spanish abandoned it in the 1830s. By the time the US seized control, the

The treeless landscape of the Lime Point Military Reservation is evident in this 1890s snapshot of hikers exploring the Needles— prominent rocks along the edge of Fort Baker's Horseshoe Bay.

forlorn castillo was a melted adobe ruin with its cannon lying on the ground.

In November 1850, a joint US Army–Navy board announced a sweeping plan for the defense of San Francisco that centered on the narrow, cliff-lined opening to the harbor. Board members recommended that two large forts be constructed at the entrance to the bay, one on either side of the strait that had recently become known as the Golden Gate. One fort would be located at Fort Point in the Presidio (named by the Americans for the ruined Spanish castillo that had once commanded the point) while a near-twin fort would be built at Lime Point on the Marin shore, a mile away. Together, these forts would able to focus the gunfire of nearly three hundred cannon at the narrowest part of the Golden Gate's strait, hammering an enemy vessel from both sides with an iron hailstorm of shot and shell.

To provide backup for these forts, the board also proposed additional gun emplacements for Alcatraz Island, where batteries positioned at each end of the island could control shipping channels through the inner harbor.

The type of forts envisioned by the army's engineers were multi-tiered masonry structures of a design already in use at harbors along the East and Gulf Coasts. Sometimes referred to as "works," these forts had cannon mounted on several tiers. Most of the guns fired through armored openings in the walls, called "embrasures," while additional cannon were mounted on the roof "en barbette" in exposed, open air emplacements.

In 1853, army engineers began work on the masonry fort slated for Fort Point and the batteries at either end of Alcatraz Island. There was no problem acquiring title to either site, as both the Presidio and Alcatraz had long been under government ownership, first by the Spanish, then the Mexicans and finally, the US. The site of the proposed Lime Point fort, however, was private property. This was going to cause serious headaches for the government.

Lime Point was still part of Rancho Saucelito, and had been in private ownership since 1838 when William Richardson received title from the Mexican government. His claim was reconfirmed by US courts in 1854, meaning that before any plans to fortify Lime Point could move ahead, the property would have to be acquired from Richardson, either

through purchase or condemnation.

While negotiations with Richardson dragged on, the army began their surveys of the Lime Point Reservation. One of the earliest descriptions of the future Fort Baker was reported in 1855 by Colonel of Engineers René De Russy: "The head lands, from Point Bonita to Lime Point, are generally abrupt on the sea-side, and of a rock formation, and yet the valleys intervening and their summits are covered with a natural growth of the country, the wild oats, which afford good pasturage during the whole year."

Other American visitors, more familiar with forested East Coast landscapes and lush farmlands, failed to see the natural beauty of these rugged Marin hills. Another army surveyor considered Lime Point's value to be "little or nothing for agriculture or grazing." Several military reports included similar descriptions of a rugged terrain: "Nothing grows upon it but grass and flowers," and "the land is broken and high; it is grazed upon by cattle and horses."

Discussions between the federal government and Richardson continued throughout the 1850s, and were further complicated in 1856, when Richardson transferred Rancho Saucelito to Samuel Throckmorton, who turned out to be an even tougher negotiator. It took ten more years of correspondence, bargaining, offers and counteroffers before the government finally reached a mutually agreeable sale price with Throckmorton.

On July 24, 1866, the government took title to the Lime Point Military Reservation, comprising 1,898.66 acres stretching from Point Cavallo to Point Bonita, and north to Rodeo Valley. The cost of the land was $125,000 (equivalent to about $950 per acre in today's dollars).

San Francisco Bay, 1853. Deserted ships, abandoned by their crews in the frenzy of the Gold Rush, crowd the harbor.

The Fort That Never Was

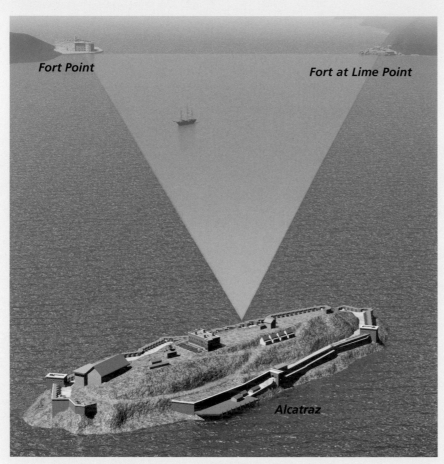

Fort Point

Fort at Lime Point

Alcatraz

Had the fort at Lime Point been built, the Golden Gate entrance would have been protected by cannon fire from three major fortifications (a "triangle of defense"). Only Fort Point and Alcatraz Island were completed, though, and were extensively fortified during the Civil War.

Incorporating many of the Corps of Engineers' standardized design features, the fort at Lime Point would have featured two tiers of cannon mounted in casemates (gun rooms) and an open-air barbette battery atop the roof that provided all-around fields of fire. Behind the casemates, two tiers of barracks, mess halls, and storerooms would have supported the hundreds of war-time soldiers needed to fire the fort's guns.

This artist's recreation (opposite) shows how the fort would have looked, based on plans approved by the army in 1867 after earlier designs were rejected. If work had actually begun, it's likely the fort's appearance would have been altered during construction.

Naming the Golden Gate

The name Golden Gate has nothing to do with gold. Instead, the evocative label was first used by controversial US explorer and army officer John C. Fremont, who likened the dramatic, cliff-lined entrance to the harbor narrows at Constantinople (ancient Byzantium) in Turkey, a strait called the "Golden Horn."

In his memoirs, Fremont recalled that he first saw the bay's mouth on July 1, 1846, while crossing the straits in a rowboat to attack the Presidio during the Mexican War: "To this Gate I gave the name of *Chrysopylae*, or 'Golden Gate'; for the same reasons that the harbor of Byzantium was called *Chrysoceras*, or Golden Horn."

If it had been built, the fort at Lime Point would have been located exactly where the north tower of the Golden Gate Bridge now stands. These illustrations, along with the one on page 13, are based on plans prepared by US Army engineers in 1867.

Below: This superimposition shows the relationship of the Golden Gate Bridge (completed in 1937) to the never-built fort at Lime Point.

Opposite: Looking from the roof of the proposed Lime Point Fort across to Fort Point on the southern shore.

Looking south along Horseshoe Cove toward the Engineers' pier and the road to Lime Point, 1869; the Needles are at left.

Chapter Three
The First Fortifications: 1867 to 1897

Work finally began in 1867 on the long-delayed casemated fort at the tip of Lime Point. Although never completed, this fort would have mounted 109 cannon in a two-story masonry structure facing Fort Point on the southern side of the gate. Construction of the fort would have required carving out a four-acre plateau at the very tip of Lime Point, a promontory rising over 400 feet straight up from the Golden Gate. Within a few months, Major George Mendell of the Corps of Engineers had workers begin the task of leveling the end of the point. Mendell estimated that it would require an excavation of 1,000,000 cubic yards to clear enough space for the fort's foundations. And it would be an expensive job, with a total projected cost of $3 million (nearly $45 million in today's dollars).

As it turned out, Major Mendell's work on the new fort was limited to establishing a work camp and some preliminary tunneling, and blasting on the east face of Lime Point. The project was doomed before it was begun, a victim of changing military technology.

Immediately following the Civil War, the US Army's Board of Engineers began reviewing the nation's existing fortifications in light of lessons hard-won during the war, especially about the vulnerability of multi-tiered forts to land-based artillery. At siege after siege, hulking masonry forts had proven themselves to be little more than oversized targets for modern, long-range artillery. (In 1862, Fort Pulaski in Georgia had come under Union artillery fire and fell after only thirty

hours of bombardment.) The army realized it needed to radically redesign all its present and future forts. For San Francisco Bay, the engineers determined that not only was the just-completed fort at Fort Point already obsolete, but also that it would be futile to build an additional fort of the same type at Lime Point. All work was halted.

In 1869, the Corps of Engineers declared a radically new design for existing and future harbor-defense forts. The new American fortifications would be low-slung affairs, constructed mostly of earth and rising only a dozen feet or so above grade when viewed from the sea. Rather than mounting cannon within masonry casemates or in long lines in open-air batteries, the army planned to emplace guns in pairs, with each pair separated from its neighbors by artificial earth hills called "traverses." The traverses would both protect against incoming enemy shells and limit battle damage to, at most, two weapons at a time. Each traverse would also incorporate an underground powder magazine to store ammunition for adjacent guns. Standardized plans were soon developed for these emplacements and traverses, which could be strung along shorelines as far as necessary to defend harbor entrances.

The guns for these new earthwork batteries were holdovers from the Civil War—cast-iron mortars and cannon able to fire cannon balls distances of more than three miles. The largest of these weapons were the 15-inch caliber Rodman guns (named

Battery Cavallo, 1902, looking toward the bay and San Francisco.

The carefully designed earthworks of Battery Cavallo as viewed from the air, 1938. Also visible are the concrete gun positions of of Battery Yates (built in 1905) at upper right.

after their War Department designer) capable of firing either an explosive shell or a solid iron shot weighing 440 pounds that could crush an ironclad warship with its meteoric impact. The army realized that newer weapon technologies were on the horizon, so provisions were made in the earthwork-battery designs for future modifications as artillery designs evolved.

At Lime Point, Mendell suspended excavations for the obsolescent multitiered fort and ordered surveys of the nearby hills carried out for locations of replacement earthwork batteries. Due to the hilly topography of the new Lime Point Military Reservation, it would prove difficult to establish the extended lines of emplacements that were being envisioned for East Coast flatlands. Instead, Mendell decided to locate them at widely separated areas along the bluffs overlooking the Golden Gate. Five sites were eventually chosen: Lime Point Ridge, above the cancelled fort's location; Point Cavallo, near Yellow Bluff on the opposite side of Horseshoe Cove; Gravelly Beach, in a sheltered valley just west of Lime Point; and at Points Diablo and Bonita even farther to the west. The new batteries would mount 74 weapons, including 13-inch mortars, 15-inch and 20-inch Rodman smoothbore guns, and (eventually) large rifles still being designed.

Mendell's first job was to build roads connecting these remote locations. By early 1870, laborers were busily constructing a network that began at the Engineers' Camp and snaked up to the summit of Lime Point Ridge and then down to Gravelly Beach. In the other

The Engineers' Camp at Lime Point, 1869. The two-story building at left was a dormitory for construction workers. Smaller buildings served as offices, warehouses and workshops.

direction, a road led to Point Cavallo, where the largest of the planned gun batteries would be built: an elegantly shaped, enclosed earthen fort with positions for fifteen cannon aimed toward the Presidio and Alcatraz Island.

As soon as the roads were finished, work crews began grading the battery sites and erecting the masonry portions of the emplacements and their adjacent underground powder magazines. Mendell considered the Point Cavallo battery especially important. Guns mounted on this promontory would cover not only the Golden Gate but also the inner bay to intersect with batteries in the Presidio, Point San Jose (also known Black Point and located at modern-day Fort Mason), Alcatraz Island and Angel Island. Mendell stressed that guns on the planned battery's left flank could cover the important anchorage off Sausalito in Richardson's Bay as well. In addition to the main battery, he recommended that a small, two-gun "outwork" be placed at the very tip of Point Cavallo to protect Horseshoe Cove.

Given the remote location of Mendell's batteries in the undeveloped Marin hills, it's understandable that construction work dragged on for years. Further hindering construction was the Chief of Engineer's requirement that every plan and drawing prepared by the San Francisco engineers be sent back to Washington, D.C., for review. This process of sending, reviewing, approving, modifying and returning every drawing could take months. At Point Cavallo, for example, Mendell submitted plans for building this critical battery in spring of 1870, but construction didn't actually get underway until two years later.

San Francisco's obsolete defenses weren't unique; similar construction was taking place at virtually every other American seaport, where aging harbor defenses were being replaced by earthwork batteries of this new design. But Congress was wearying of the seemingly endless requests by the War Department for more allocations for fortifications, especially in the aftermath of the bloody and costly Civil War. Additionally, lawmakers remembered that the recent war had shown masonry defenses to be obsolescent, and wondered how long before this expensive new system of earthworks also became outmoded.

As a result, Congress took draconian measures. Across the nation, fortification construction came to a complete halt on June 30, 1876. That year, Congress allocated only a very small annual sum (roughly $100,000 nationwide) for maintenance of completed fortifications. No more new work was authorized, despite the fact that most of the nation's completed batteries still lacked their armament.

Lime Point and all of the unfinished fortifications were relegated to caretaker status for the next two decades. Although the batteries at Cavallo Point, Lime Ridge and Gravelly Beach were physically complete, no work had even been started at Point Diablo or Point Bonita. The situation at Cavallo Battery was typical: the unarmed battery stood 95 percent complete, lacking finishing touches such as masonry platforms and parapet walls for the Rodman guns.

Throughout the Lime Point Reservation, only a single cannon had ever been mounted in the finished emplacements, a lonely 15-inch Rodman gun at Gravelly Beach. The closest artillerymen who could fire the weapon were at Fort Point on the other side of the Golden Gate.

With little budget for maintenance, the earthworks soon fell into disrepair. All around the bay, erosion and encroaching brush and trees began to obliterate the batteries. Even the wildlife at Lime Point was taking its toll on the empty emplacements. In one of his annual reports, Mendell wrote: "A little rodent called the Gopher is the worst enemy we have. He burrows in the parapets and destroys their shape and compactness." Poisoning the critters did not help because, complained Mendell, "recruits from outlying country come in."

America's harbor defenses, and indeed the country's entire military readiness, declined for another decade as the United States slumped in stature as a military power. But perhaps this was a blessing in disguise, because while American forts went unarmed and gophers munched on Mendell's earthworks, European powers continued to fight wars and simultaneously improve fortification and artillery designs. Across the Atlantic, forged-steel guns began to replace those made of cast iron, and armor plate and concrete superseded brick and granite for fort materials. When America finally began upgrading its fleets and fortifications, it would draw heavily on these advances in European war technology.

In 1885, Secretary of War William Endicott convened a long-overdue board to review the sad state of American

Lime Point viewed from the Presidio, about 1890, with Fort Point in the foreground. The white buildings at the foot of the ridge make up the Lime Point Fog Signal Station. At the top of the ridge, two small mounds indicate the location of Cliff Battery overlooking the Golden Gate.

A typical 1870s earthwork battery consisted of pairs of Rodman cannon separated by artificial earthen hills. The doorway at right led to an underground ammunition magazine.

Battery Spencer, completed in 1897, was the first of the Endicott-era batteries built at Fort Baker. It occupied the site of the former Cliff Battery.

defenses and make recommendations for improving the nation's forts. The board's sweeping proposals would result in a wholesale rebuilding of American fortifications and become the basis for the next generation of construction, which extended from 1890 to 1905.

In 1886, the board made its report, calling for extensive new fortification projects at twenty-six American coastal locales. Recommendations ran the gamut from gun batteries and mortars to patrol boats and underwater minefields. In general, the Endicott Board recommended emplacing several calibers of guns ranging from 12-inch rifles and mortars designed to deal with heavily armored battleships and cruisers down to 3-inch rapid-fire guns meant to take on swift motor torpedo and patrol boats.

The Endicott Board's initial vision for the defense of San Francisco was ambitious, proposing scores of new weapons and electrically controlled underwater minefields to protect the shipping channels, making it the second most heavily defended port in the country after New York. The new generation of weaponry would be mounted on radically new styles of carriages, including rotating armored turrets, hydraulic gun lifts and disappearing carriages. (The latter used the gun's recoil force to lower the weapon downward behind a parapet after each shot while simultaneously raising a lead counterweight, in effect, making it "disappear" from view. When the gun was reloaded, the weight was released and the gun rose back up to firing position.)

Not all recommendations were implemented—no turrets or gun lifts were ever constructed in San Francisco—but the general direction of the bay's new defenses had been established. The region's "Endicott Era" fortifications would feature steel breech-loading artillery pieces in a variety of calibers, all firing elongated pointed projectiles with ranges upwards of ten miles. Gun emplacements and magazines would now be constructed of poured concrete, dozens of feet thick in places, surrounded by even greater thicknesses of earthen fill. Heavy shells and powder would be raised to the surface on elevators for loading.

Construction on the Endicott batteries at Lime Point Military Reservation began in the mid-1890s at five locations spread along the Marin shore as recommended by engineer Mendell (see box).

Some of these fortified sites remained strategically important throughout the evolution of the bay's harbor defenses. Batteries Spencer and Kirby actually occupied the same real estate as some of Mendell's never-completed 1870s batteries, and their new construction nearly obliterated the old earthwork emplacements. During World War II, both sites would be fortified once again, this time with rapid-fire anti-torpedo-boat and anti-aircraft guns.

A 15-inch caliber Rodman cannon mounted on an iron carriage. Wheels at the rear of the carriage allowed the 73,000 pound weapon to be manually pivoted (traversed) through 180 degrees.

Battery Name	Weapons	Location
Spencer	Three 12-inch rifles on barbette carriages	Atop Lime Point ridge
Kirby	Two 12-inch rifles on disappearing carriages	Gravelly Beach
Duncan	Two 8-inch rifles on barbette carriages	Atop hill overlooking Cavallo Point
Wagner	Two 5-inch rapid-fire rifles	On road to Gravelly Beach
Yates	Six 3-inch rapid-fire rifles	Cavallo Point

The First Guns

When construction began on the Endicott batteries in the 1890s, the first guns mounted on the Marin side as defensive weapons were actually four Civil War-era Rodmans moved from the Presidio of San Francisco and placed in the empty 1870s positions on Lime Point Ridge. Given the downward-angled fire they could bring to an attacking ship's decks, these aging cannon were still considered potent weapons. Emplaced in 1892, the four guns provided interim protection to the Marin shore while workers constructed larger and more complex concrete emplacements for 12-inch rifled guns at the end of the ridge. (A single Rodman cannon had been mounted at Gravelly Beach in 1873, but it was installed to test a proposed gun mount rather than as part of the bay's defenses.)

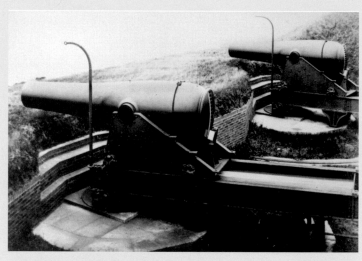

Ridge Battery showing two of the four Rodman guns mounted there in 1893. The army brought over these aging—but still effective— 15-inch guns from the Presidio to defend Lime Point while nearby Battery Spencer was under construction.

Opposite, top: 12-inch caliber rifle on a barbette carriage, Model 1892. Guns of this style could fire a half-ton shell over eight miles, and were designed to duel with heavily armored battleships and battlecruisers.

Opposite, bottom: Battery O'Rorke near Point Bonita and its four rapid-firing 3-inch caliber guns, about 1907. Small caliber weapons like these were designed to fire light 15-pound shells at a very rapid rate— sometimes as quickly as once every three seconds. O'Rorke's guns were also sited to protect against a beach landing.

Although never fired in anger, San Francisco's coastal artillery guns were fired regularly during target practices.

Who Was the Enemy?

The Endicott program's stout emplacements would survive long after the guns were dismounted. Many modern-day visitors to the empty gun emplacements at Fort Baker speculate that the army built the batteries as a wartime response to imminent enemy attack, probably during World War II. In fact, most of the aging emplacements were built much earlier, with the majority at Fort Baker constructed between 1896 and 1905. And they weren't built in response to actual hostilities but rather, during peacetime, in anticipation of the day the country did go to war.

But if we weren't at war, who was the perceived enemy a century ago? A September 29, 1897, story in the *San Francisco Call* described the potential foes:

> Army and navy officers fancy that the harbor defenses are now sufficiently well advanced to stand off any fleet that Spain or Japan could put into action here. England is the great power that we may be called on to fight at the entrance of the Golden Gate. She has a station at Vancouver, where her fleets may assemble and outfit for operations against San Francisco. Our position is strong enough …to make a splendid fight against the best fleet England could send against us.

The Lime Point Fog Signal Station

Just as the army constructed a ring of forts around the Golden Gate, the US Lighthouse Board established a network of lighthouses and fog signals around San Francisco Bay. One of these, a pair of steam-powered fog whistles, was constructed in 1883 at the very tip of Lime Point on a narrow finger of rock barely twenty feet wide. Its purpose was simple: warn ships away from the rocky northern shore of the Golden Gate.

When complete, the tiny station included a brick building that housed steam boilers and two 12-inch-diameter steam whistles. An adjacent two-story residence provided housing for the two lighthouse keepers who maintained the station.

The hungry boilers consumed coal at a rate of 250 pounds per hour during foggy weather, when the steam whistles operated non-stop. Coal and all other supplies had to be transported across a treacherous, narrow trail along the foot of Lime Point that was often blocked by rockslides clattering down the cliffs.

The station grew over the years. In 1900, a light was installed on the outside of the boiler house, turning Lime Point into a full-fledged lighthouse and fog station. A third keeper was added to the staff, and a third story added to the keepers' residence. Storehouses and workshops sprouted along the shore near the station building. In 1923, the keepers were given the additional responsibility of maintaining a tiny light placed on Point Diablo, a mile west of Lime Point. Then, in 1939, the Lighthouse Service keepers became members of the US Coast Guard when the two agencies merged.

Life at the station was usually uneventful, but there was occasional excitement. The 1906 earthquake caused extensive slides along the trail, which isolated Lime Point from the rest of Fort Baker, and one night in 1960, the steam ship *India Bear* wandered off course and rammed into the station, even though the fog signal was sounding. The ship sustained $60,000 worth of damage, while the station had a repair bill of only $7,500.

But the most unusual event must have been a night in December 1959, when the station was held up by an armed gunman. The robber ordered the Coast Guardsmen to hand over their cash, fired a few warning shots into the air, then disappeared down the station's narrow road.

Lime Point was automated in July 1961 and the keepers' quarters and outbuildings were torn down shortly thereafter, leaving only the original brick boiler house visible today. Though the station no longer displays a light, it continues to serve as a Coast Guard fog signal, one which now employs a high-tech electronic klaxon to warn vessels away from its still lime-covered rocks.

The Lime Point station its height, circa 1958. The long wing at left housed the fog signal and light beacon, and the three-story central section was the keepers' residence. The immense base of the Golden Gate Bridge's north tower is at upper left.

FORT BAKER
SAN FRANCISCO HARBOR
CALIFORNIA

SCALE: 1 INCH - 400 FEET

NOTES

SERIAL PRINT N° 8.
1ST SAN FRANCISCO DISTRICT.

DRAWING NO. 19

Chapter Four
A Harbor Defense Fort: 1897 to 1937

QUARTERS AT FORT BAKER, CAL.

Although the army acquired the Lime Point Military Reservation in 1866, it took more than thirty years to begin stationing soldiers there.

Throughout the first decades of fortification construction, abandonment and reconstruction, all military operations at Lime Point were under the control of the US Army Corps of Engineers. Following standard procedure, regular troops didn't move into a fort until the batteries were completed and formally transferred to the Artillery branch. When construction was suspended at Lime Point in 1876, the batteries hadn't yet received their armament, so there was no need for troops or living quarters. By 1897, though, work had resumed and the first of the Endicott batteries was nearing completion.

On May 4, 1897, the Lime Point Military Reservation was officially named in honor of former Senator Edward D. Baker of Oregon (see page 38). As the new emplacements at Fort Baker were nearing completion, the army began making plans to station a permanent garrison of troops at the freshly minted post.

Within about two months, soldiers began arriving at Fort Baker to take up guard duties around the gun emplacements and maintain the 12-inch and 15-inch guns that had just been mounted. These soldiers, who were from Battery I of the Third US Artillery, were shipped over from nearby Camp

Reynolds on Angel Island in July 1897. (Over the decades, US Army units assigned to the artillery branch have alternately been called "batteries" or "companies" of men. These units usually numbered about 100 enlisted soldiers during the 1890s.)

The army had long planned for a permanent post in the sheltered valley north of Horseshoe Cove, one that would include barracks, officers' quarters, a hospital and other support structures facing a spacious, grassy parade ground. However, the construction of such complexes (sometimes called garrison or cantonment areas) was the responsibility of the army's Quartermaster Department, not the Engineers, and no progress had been made on this ambitious project when the soldiers from Company I arrived. Instead, the artillerymen were quartered in tents during their first foggy summer at the fort.

That fall, the soldiers received more permanent accommodations when a pair of wooden barracks were barged over

Opposite: A 1916 map of Fort Baker shows the main post buildings surrounding the semicircular parade ground. Also visible are the gun batteries at Cavallo Point, Lime Point and Kirby Cove.

Above: An early postcard view of the parade ground with a treeless landscape and fog lurking over the Marin hills.

Battery Duncan

View from Battery Spencer 1902

Angel Island

Ft Baker

Pt Cavallo Battery

Horse shoe Bay

Lime Point

An annotated photograph of Fort Baker and "Horse Shoe Bay," 1902. The marshy area above the two-masted schooner was a tidal wetland, considered to be a health hazard by the post's doctor. It was filled the following year.

from the Presidio of San Francisco and rebuilt near the shore of Horseshoe Cove. At that time, the future parade ground site was still a natural valley known as Old Ranch Valley, with a creek running down its middle. Much work needed to be done to create a parade ground and the permanent cantonment around it, so the two temporary barracks—along with a stable, corral and guardhouse—were located in a north-south row at the edge of the sloping valley.

At the time, a tidal wetland extended in from the bayshore not far from where the barracks were located, between today's marina and the coast guard station, and its presence caused all manner of grief for the early military tenants. One post surgeon dramatically described the small slough as little more than a cesspool where millions of germs were produced and poisonous "malarial vapors" were generated. Though higher medical authorities discounted the doctor's theory of imminent malarial hazard, plans were carried out to fill in the slough, both because it was an eyesore and to increase the area of the planned parade ground. The wetland finally disappeared in 1903—an environmental loss unthinkable today—when it was buried under 80,000 cubic yards of bay fill.

In addition to filling the wetland, the army also filled in and graded the natural valley behind it to create the expansive parade ground (or parade field) that would become the center of life at the post. At most forts, the most important buildings were arranged in a rectangle facing in toward the parade ground. Traditionally, enlisted men's barracks lined one side and officers' quarters the opposite, with the post headquarters and administrative buildings on the third. The fourth side was generally occupied by noncommissioned officers' (NCO) residences and structures such as warehouses,

In 1904 the army subdivided Fort Baker into two posts: Fort Barry on the west and Fort Baker on the east. The dividing line was Point Diablo, midway between Cavallo Point and Lime Point.

shops and a bakery. At some distance (ideally, downwind) sat the stable, corrals and wagon shed. For health reasons, the fort's hospital was traditionally located away from the parade ground and other residential areas.

Fort Baker, though, would break with this long-established layout. Instead, the anonymous military designers who laid out the post took advantage of the valley's natural setting by arranging the most important buildings in a gentle semicircle, leaving the south side open to maximize views toward San Francisco Bay and the city. In keeping with tradition, the enlisted men's barracks were built on one side and the officers' quarters across from them, while the post headquarters and the commanding officer's residence were at the head of the valley. The designers placed the NCO quarters and hospital farther up the valley north of the parade ground, while the stables, warehouses and shop buildings were sited along the bayshore at the southeast corner of the post; to keep them out of sight of the parade, they were built on an angled axis.

It was a delightful plan, but it was just a plan. Soldiers continued to live in temporary quarters at Fort Baker for several more years. It wasn't until 1900 that the army finally invited contractors to bid on constructing a cantonment of thirteen permanent garrison buildings. Initially on the list were two officers' family duplexes, a barracks for a 109-man company of enlisted soldiers, two NCO duplexes, a post hospital, hospital steward's quarters, guardhouse, bakery, quartermaster subsistence warehouse, stable, wagon room and fuel shed.

The contract for constructing the first permanent buildings was awarded in June 1901 and construction began shortly after. Almost simultaneously, the number of soldiers stationed at the post began to expand, and the number of buildings was increased to keep pace with housing needs. Before long, the post would include three barracks, a commanding

Life at Fort Baker

A soldier's life at Fort Baker differed little from life at other Coast Artillery posts of the time. Day after day, official activities followed the same monotonous pattern: morning reveille, formations, artillery drill, small-arms target practice, fatigue duties, guard duty, inspections, parades and a variety of other tasks.

Headed up by a commanding officer (CO), usually a major or colonel, each officer and enlisted soldier at Fort Baker had a part to play. The post adjutant and the sergeant major were the administrative aides of the CO, with whom they shared offices at the post headquarters on the north end of the parade ground. Most of the CO's orders were transmitted through these men. The post quartermaster officer and quartermaster sergeant were responsible for clothing, housing and supplying the garrison, while the post commissary officer and mess sergeant were responsible for feeding the men. The post surgeon, or frequently, a noncommissioned hospital steward, presided over the small hospital behind officers' row and also looked after the sanitary condition of the fort.

Soldiers at Fort Baker were initially part of the US Artillery branch, but after a 1907 army reorganization, they were integrated into the new Coast Artillery Corps. Each company of soldiers (called either a "company of Coast Artillery" or a "battery") had an authorized strength of 109 men, supposedly under the direction of a captain and two lieutenants; however, full strength was not always achieved. Though company officers could sometimes be found directing their units at the batteries, paper work in the company orderly room at the barracks consumed much of their time. Sergeants and corporals usually had direct contract with the troops, ensuring that orders from the CO and

company officers were carried out. At specified times of the day, a bugler blew appropriate calls, regulating the routine of the military community.

For diversion, the Fort Baker artillerymen had a band, a library, several sports teams, a gym and a post exchange that served as a combination lunch counter and corner store. Popular off-duty pastimes were reading, sports, gambling and sampling the pleasures of the village of Sausalito, just north of the reservation boundary. Army steamboats shuttled between the fort's wharf and downtown San Francisco, offering still greater diversions to soldiers with passes. For those men who had enjoyed city life a little too much, the post guardhouse and its iron jail cells stood ready.

Officers and their wives enjoyed a life quite different from those of the enlisted men. They lived in spacious homes facing the parade and moved in a totally different social world. Many of the officers came from distinguished families, and most were West Point graduates. By virtue of their education and background, they were considered part of San Francisco's elite social scene. Husbands and wives attended concerts and parties at Fort Baker and other army posts around the bay, and regularly traveled to San Francisco to enjoy plays, concerts, balls, the opera and other social events.

Rifle practice at Fort Baker took place virtually in the back yards of the post's buildings. The building at right in the photo above is the post hospital, making one wonder what the effect was on its patients. Uniforms and equipment indicate this undated target practice likely took place during World War I.

Sports at the Fort

Military posts in the 1900s actively encouraged a variety of sports programs, including baseball, basketball, football and boxing. Sports provided a healthy outlet for the energies of young men confined to a military post and encouraged competition between the companies and regiments that manned the harbor defenses of San Francisco.

Fort Baker teams competed with nearby army posts as well as civilian teams and high schools and colleges. (In one notorious matchup, the Fort Baker football team lost to the Stanford University varsity, 57-0.)

Fort Baker's football and baseball teams. Some of the football players display bent noses and bruises typical of the pre-safety equipment era. Below, the baseball players, sitting on a barracks porch, are wearing the uniform of the 61st Company of Coast Artillery. Sergeant William T. Dillon, the team captain, is at center.

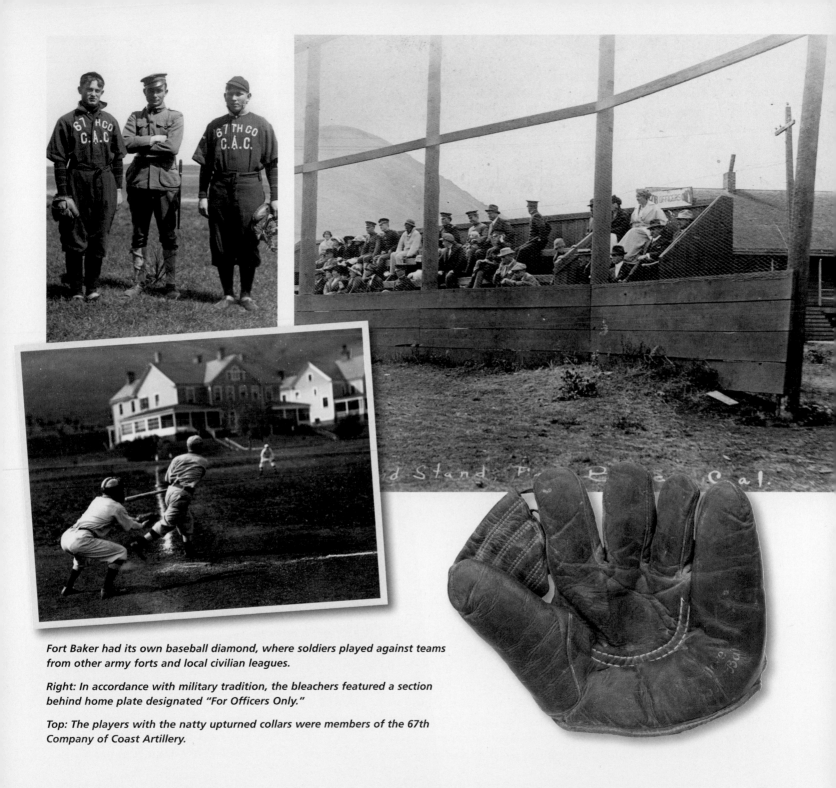

Fort Baker had its own baseball diamond, where soldiers played against teams from other army forts and local civilian leagues.

Right: In accordance with military tradition, the bleachers featured a section behind home plate designated "For Officers Only."

Top: The players with the natty upturned collars were members of the 67th Company of Coast Artillery.

officer's residence, a post headquarters building, five sets of officers' duplexes, five NCO duplexes, a 12-bed hospital, steward's residence, gymnasium, guardhouse, several warehouses, horse and mule stables, bakery, blacksmith shop, wagon sheds, and pump house.

In many ways, Fort Baker was typical in appearance of many army posts built at the time. All its buildings were based on "standard plan" architectural designs developed the US Army Quartermaster Department in Washington, D.C. The quartermasters used the same building plans around the country, whether the posts were for artillery or infantry or cavalry units; the only variety came in the choice of materials used to construct the buildings—brick or wood.

In fact, the original specifications for Fort Baker's permanent cantonment called for utilizing brick in all the buildings, but when the bids for brick construction came in too high, the earliest structures were built using economical Douglas fir and redwood. It wasn't until 1903 that affordable brick came into use at the post, and then, a new barracks, gymnasium and storehouse were constructed of the more fireproof material.

At the same time that the Quartermaster Department was overseeing the construction of the cantonment, the engineers were working on still another generation of harbor defense fortifications. These batteries represented an effort to match the size and range of the new and heavier guns that were starting to appear on enemy battleships. This time, though, the new batteries would be located not at Lime Point but at the undeveloped western end of Fort Baker, where their long-range gun fire could engage an enemy fleet far at sea.

By positioning the new batteries on the westernmost points of land in both Marin and San Francisco, enemy warships could be kept beyond a range from which they could shell the city and its harbor. To defend the San Francisco side, the army established Fort Miley above Lands End. On the Marin side, they selected a remote area of Fort Baker adjacent to the Point Bonita lighthouse and Rodeo Beach.

The Point Bonita emplacements were three miles from the rest of Fort Baker, and could only be reached by a treacherous cliffside trail that snaked over the hills west of the main post. In order to construct the new batteries, the engineers built a wharf near the lighthouse to land construction materials and

artillery pieces. Just as at Lime Point years earlier, they also established an "engineer camp" where civilian workers lived while building the batteries.

Battery Name	Weapons
Mendell	Two 12-inch rifles on disappearing carriages
Alexander	Eight 12-inch mortars
Guthrie	Four 6-inch rifles on barbette carriages
Rathbone	Four 6-inch rifles on barbette carriages
Yates	Four 3-inch rapid fire rifles

By 1903, five more gun batteries were nearing completion at the Point Bonita district (see box).

The new Point Bonita batteries and barracks were so distant from the rest of Fort Baker that the army decided to make the area its own distinct fort. This was accomplished by administratively dividing Fort Baker in half, using as reference a north-south line running through Point Diablo, midway between Lime Point and Point Bonita. On December 27, 1904, the War Department designated the new post "Fort Barry" in honor of Brigadier General William F. Barry, a colonel of the 2nd US Artillery who had died in 1879.

By the 1910s, Fort Baker was part of a chain that included Forts Winfield Scott, Miley and Funston in San Francisco; Fort McDowell on Angel Island; and Fort Barry near the Point Bonita lighthouse. Fort Baker was technically a subpost of Fort Winfield Scott in the Presidio of San Francisco, which was the headquarters for all the harbor defense posts surrounding San Francisco Bay and, later, the entire Pacific Coast.

Like many Coast Artillery posts, the army didn't garrison Fort Baker with a full complement of soldiers at all times, nor did they intend to man the fort's batteries around the clock. Military plans dictated that Coast Artillery fortifications were an investment for wartime, and the batteries and barracks areas would be kept in readiness by small contingents of soldiers during peacetime. For long intervals, many American Coast Artillery posts were actually more like well-groomed ghost towns, garrisoned only by a few caretaker

The main post at Fort Baker around 1912, looking south toward the Golden Gate. The road to Fort Barry can be seen winding up the hillside at right. Forts Baker and Barry were isolated posts at this time, accessible only by boat from San Francisco. A steamer headed for the city is waiting at the quartermaster pier at the water's edge.

Who Was Baker?

The Lime Point Military Reservation was formally named Fort Baker in General Orders No. 25 issued by the Headquarters of the US Army on May 4, 1897. The name was selected to honor Colonel Edward Dickinson Baker, who had been killed in action during the Civil War while leading the 71st Pennsylvania Infantry Regiment at the Battle of Ball's Bluff, Virginia, on October 21, 1861. A native of England, Baker had settled first in Illinois, from which he was elected to the US House of Representatives and where he developed a close friendship with a young lawyer named Abraham Lincoln. Later, he moved to California, then to Oregon, and in 1860, was elected US Senator from Oregon. He was the only sitting US Senator to be killed in action during the Civil War.

troops who lived in the barracks, maintained the grounds and buildings, and ensured the security of the gun emplacements and munitions.

When war loomed, troops were once again moved in. The army also assumed that local National Guard units, called into action during wartime, would augment the Regular Army Coast Artillery troops who maintained the fortifications.

As a result, the size of Fort Baker's garrison changed dramatically over its first few decades, sometimes comprising a full complement of more than three hundred enlisted men while at other times dropping to only a handful of caretakers. One of the high points occurred in the summer of 1909, when more than five hundred men of the 32nd, 61st, 67th, 68th and 148th companies of the Coast Artillery Corps were stationed there. At other times, records indicate that only a single company could be found at the post.

The population at Fort Baker swelled during World War I, not because of any fear of attack but as a result of an influx of trainees headed for the battlefields of Europe. Temporary encampments were established at Fort Baker and Fort Barry and in the intervening valleys of the Marin Headlands. At one point in 1918, there were nearly 6,000 troops at Forts Baker and Barry.

Following the end of the Great War, troop levels again dropped off. Between 1922 and 1931, Fort Baker was predominately occupied by caretaker units from Fort Scott in the Presidio. All of the Bay Area's forts were similarly reduced to caretaker status as the nation demilitarized during the 1920s and military preparedness continued to decline during the Great Depression of the 1930s.

The lack of a full garrison didn't mean the fort went unused, though. Coast Artillery from the Presidio and California National Guard units drilled regularly at Fort Baker's gun batteries, and the caretaker units provided regular maintenance of the fortifications and the post buildings.

An aerial photograph of Fort Baker, 1925. Ornamental trees planted as windbreaks are now well established. The cluster of buildings at lower right was the quartermaster's complex of shops, storehouses, bakery, stables, and other support structures. The portal to the new Baker-Barry tunnel is at upper center.

605
Officers' Duplex

606
Officers' Duplex

607
Officers' Duplex

629
Officers' Duplex

631
Officers' Duplex

McReynolds Road

Murray Circle

604
Commanding
Officer's House

Main Parade Ground

Innovations in Army Post Life

The design and architecture of Fort Baker were
departures from earlier western military forts.
Fort Baker was a new model, one in which both
the enlisted soldiers and the officers enjoyed a
much higher standard of living.

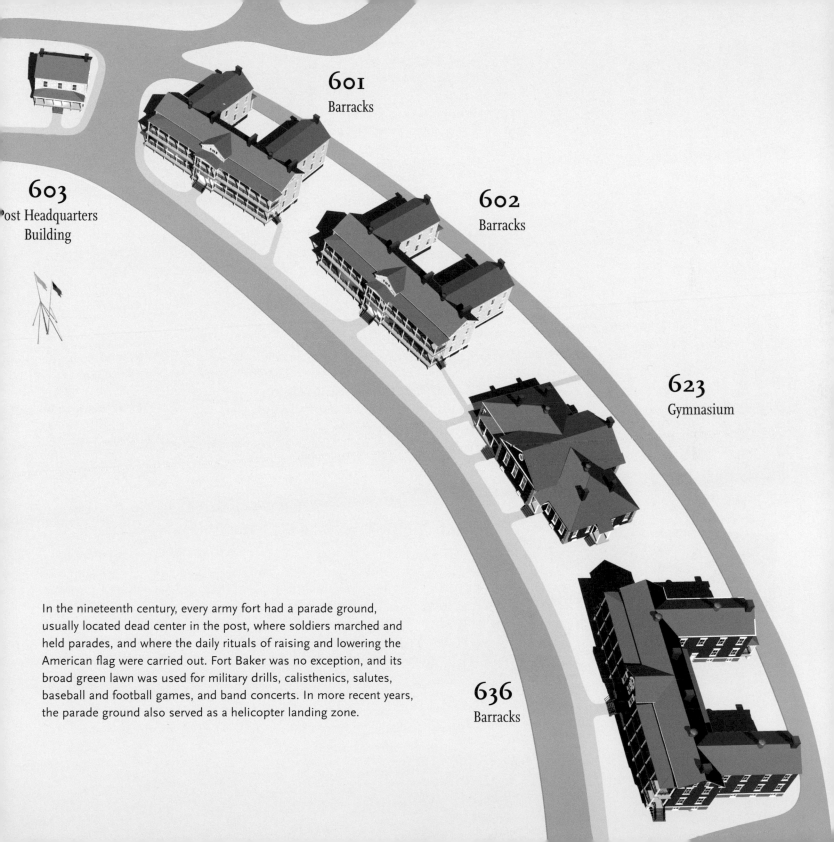

601
Barracks

603
Post Headquarters
Building

602
Barracks

623
Gymnasium

In the nineteenth century, every army fort had a parade ground, usually located dead center in the post, where soldiers marched and held parades, and where the daily rituals of raising and lowering the American flag were carried out. Fort Baker was no exception, and its broad green lawn was used for military drills, calisthenics, salutes, baseball and football games, and band concerts. In more recent years, the parade ground also served as a helicopter landing zone.

636
Barracks

To appreciate the significance of this change, it helps to understand the challenges of routine army life during the late nineteenth century preceding the establishment of Fort Baker. The soldiers' work was often both physically demanding and tedious, and their military pay allowed for few luxuries. The small frontier posts were a collection of drafty, run-down barracks that were poorly ventilated and lacked running water, separate bathrooms or electricity. The food was generally poor quality and in short supply, and the soldiers' uniforms were made of shoddy, ill-fitting material. It is easy to understand why encouraging responsible men to join the army was a challenge. Many who enlisted felt they had no other choice—they often were either in trouble with the law or flat-out broke.

WE NEED YOU!
COAST ARTILLERY CORPS U.S.A.

But much of this miserable life changed during the last years of the nineteenth century as the army turned its energy toward improving the living conditions of enlisted soldiers. This, it was hoped, would stem desertion, boost morale and attract a better class of recruits. Fort Baker was designed and built at the time the army was instituting these new policies. By the turn of the century, the army was taking a new approach to military architecture, and these changes can be easily identified at Fort Baker. Following are a few highlights of its architectural history.

BUILDING 615, GUARDHOUSE

The guardhouse was the central security post for Fort Baker. Soldiers were assigned to guard duty in twenty-four-hour shifts, during which they stood sentry around the fort and remained on stand-by in case of emergencies. The forward part of the building held a guard room, where sentries relaxed and slept between standing post, and an office for the Officer of the Day, who commanded the guard detail. The guardhouse also served as the fort's jail, and the back room had several cells in which unruly soldiers were confined while awaiting disciplinary hearings or undergoing punishment. (Short sentences were usually served here in the guardhouse. Soldiers convicted of serious crimes were sent to the army's Disciplinary Barracks on Alcatraz to serve long sentences.)

Four companies of Coast Artillery soldiers stand at attention on the Fort Baker parade ground, circa 1910. Newly planted trees (probably blue gum eucalyptus and Monterey cypress) are visible behind the duplex houses of Officers' Row. These saplings would soon grow into effective windbreaks, protecting the buildings from the westerly winds blowing across the Marin hills.

602
Barracks

623
Gymnasium

BUILDING 623, POST GYMNASIUM

In addition to raising the soldiers' pay and providing new uniforms, the army also began to sponsor facilities and activities to help alleviate the monotony of army life. The post exchange system, which offered soldiers recreation, beer and general dry goods at a fair price, was established. The army placed new emphasis on physical activity, and in addition to the formation of baseball teams, football teams and marching bands, most new army posts included some kind of gymnasium space. The army also provided teachers, textbooks and libraries to help educate the men.

The Fort Baker gymnasium originally featured a fully equipped exercise facility with basketball courts, climbing ropes, vault horses, flying rings, tumbling mats and punching bags. Much of the equipment was manufactured by the Narragansett Machine Company; when some of the the exercise machines were found many years later, the company's logo was still visible on their wooden bases. The gymnasium also included a schoolroom and library, a post exchange, a lunch counter and kitchen, and a bowling alley.

636
Barracks

BUILDING 636, ENLISTED SOLDIERS' BARRACKS

All of Fort Baker's historic barracks represented "state-of-the-art" military housing when they were completed in 1903. In Building 636, 109 soldiers lived, slept, ate, barbered and bathed. Earlier military housing had been quite different. During the late 1800s, army medical officers had been appalled at the soldiers' living conditions. Two to three men would often share one bug-ridden, makeshift bed in a damp and cramped barrack. Many posts provided only one bathtub for fifty men; it was not uncommon for the men to bathe no more than once a month.

All this changed in the 1900s, as the army began to design larger, healthier barracks with a new emphasis on proper ventilation; clean, running water; and modern toilet facilities. The Fort Baker barracks were designed with open, spacious squad rooms, numerous windows, and real beds and mattresses. All were equipped with electricity, hot and cold running water, and a sufficient number of proper toilets and shower facilities. The first floor comprised a large kitchen, mess hall (communal dining room) and day room (recreation and reading room). In the dormitories, which were located on the first and second floors, the enlisted soldiers slept in large, open rooms while NCOs, usually unmarried sergeants and corporals, slept in private rooms. The bathroom facilities were in the basement and each barracks building had its own tailor shop and barbershop.

601
Barracks

602
Barracks

BUILDINGS 601 AND 602, BARRACKS

These two historic barracks, like most of Fort Baker's buildings constructed between 1902 and 1910, were designed in the Colonial Revival architectural style. The goal of this style, which favored clean, simple lines and a minimal use of applied decoration, was to inspire a sentimental remembrance of the early history of the United States, a time when American democracy was in its infancy.

The Colonial Revival style is often characterized by large, stocky symmetrical buildings with classical elements, such as columns, porches and wide windows. At Fort Baker, the buildings were originally painted in dark greens and browns and had gray slate roofs. By the 1930s, in an effort to match other Bay Area army posts, such as the Presidio, the army repainted the post's buildings an off-white color and replaced the slate roofs with red asphalt shingles. All three barracks were originally constructed with two-story front porches, which were removed in the 1950s. When the buildings were renovated in 2006, the porches on Buildings 601 and 602 were restored.

KOBER STREET, NCO HOUSING

Modest, noncommissioned officers' duplex housing lines each side of Kober Street; the homes' scale and location reflect the lower rank of their occupants. While the officer class (lieutenants, captains and majors) lived in large duplexes facing directly on the parade ground, the NCOs and their families lived in smaller residences away from the heart of the post. Nonetheless, it was a privilege to have families on the post; lower-ranking married soldiers had to find housing for their families off-post.

Though most of the Fort Baker buildings are wood-frame construction, Kober Street's two brick buildings are the only masonry residences. A nearby single-family residence (Building 522) was constructed specifically for the Fort Baker hospital steward.

BUILDING 533, POST HOSPITAL

The Fort Baker Hospital was constructed in 1902 as a 12-bed facility. Changes in the army medical health care system were also apparent at Fort Baker. Before the turn of the century, sick soldiers were treated in drafty, temporary buildings. If their post did not have a surgeon assigned to it, they often had to wait long intervals for the traveling doctor to visit. Inadequate sleeping, sanitation and bathing facilities meant that diseases such as smallpox, yellow fever and cholera were an unfortunately common part of army life.

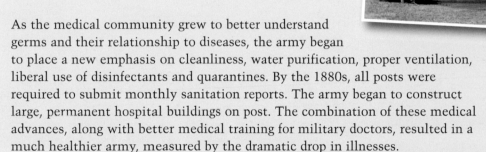

As the medical community grew to better understand germs and their relationship to diseases, the army began to place a new emphasis on cleanliness, water purification, proper ventilation, liberal use of disinfectants and quarantines. By the 1880s, all posts were required to submit monthly sanitation reports. The army began to construct large, permanent hospital buildings on post. The combination of these medical advances, along with better medical training for military doctors, resulted in a much healthier army, measured by the dramatic drop in illnesses.

Fort Baker's hospital had a medical store room and vegetable cellar in the basement and an open, well-ventilated ward room, medicine dispensary, kitchen and mess hall on the first floor. The second floor housed an operating room, a laboratory and an isolation ward for those with communicable diseases.

As Fort Baker never saw battle, this modest post hospital primarily served as a dispensary, with its doctors treating routine illnesses and providing emergency medical care. Seriously ill or injured soldiers were transported to nearby Letterman General Hospital in the Presidio of San Francisco, the largest army hospital in the west.

604
Commanding
Officer's Quarters

603
Post Headquarters
Building

BUILDING 604,
COMMANDING OFFICER'S QUARTERS

At all military posts, the commanding officer's residence was intentionally sited in a very prominent location, as it is at Fort Baker. This residence, built in 1903, originally had seven bedrooms and four bathrooms, and was designed as the largest single-family house on the post. It also incorporated embellishments such as pressed-metal ceilings, fireplaces with decorative mantels and a built-in buffet in the dining room.

With its formal dining room, living room and library, it was also designed for social functions. The commanding officer and his wife were expected to host a variety of parties and dinners for visiting military dignitaries. These large social events could not have been possible without the help of servants; the servant quarters were located on the third floor, and the residence had a separate servant's staircase in the rear.

BUILDING 603, POST HEADQUARTERS

Constructed in 1903, Building 603 contained offices for both the commanding officer and his adjutant, who was responsible for the post's administrative functions, including maintaining correspondence and records. The post headquarters also consisted of clerks' offices, a court-martial room and a reading room.

Who were the men stationed at Fort Baker? The 1910 census of Fort Baker provides us with valuable information. Most of the enlisted men were in their twenties; unmarried; and from the northern, western and midwestern states. The unmarried enlisted men claimed professions such as cooks, tailors, musicians and mechanics; the married NCOs and officers were identified simply by rank as majors, sergeants and captains. Unlike the earlier frontier army, which consisted in large part of recent immigrants, most of the Fort Baker men in 1910 were second- and third-generation Americans; only about one out of every fifteen soldiers was from another country. Places of origin included Germany, Poland, Sweden, Ireland, England, Portugal, Austria and Hungary. African-Americans were not allowed in the Coast Artillery until the eve of World War II.

Army recruitment offices around the country posted "wanted" signs in hope of enticing men into joining. Why did they enlist during peacetime? Civilian life did not always offer job security; rises in unemployment often influenced men to enlist because they saw the army as a secure job when other possibilities did not exist. Many men wanted adventure—to ride horses and see the West. Some joined the army to gain an education, with the hope of advancement.

631
Officers' Duplex

629
Officers' Duplex

607
Officers' Duplex

606
Officers' Duplex

605
Officers' Duplex

BUILDINGS 631 TO 605, OFFICERS' HOUSING

Before Fort Baker was established, frontier outposts were predominantly bachelor societies. The army strongly discouraged married junior officers, and enlisted soldiers were specifically forbidden to marry (though many of them did anyway). Officers' wives and children were to be left behind, but if they were determined to follow their husbands and fathers, the army made no provision for them. As a result, several groups of families and servants were often forced to live together in makeshift housing in deteriorating or abandoned buildings.

But by the turn of the century, as part of the effort to improve morale, officers were allowed to bring their families with them. Residences along Officers' Row were constructed in 1902–1904 for lieutenant, captain and majors' families. These large homes and the others along Officers' Row, with their ornate dining rooms, elegant living rooms and numerous bedrooms, became the new model for family life on post. Each accommodated a large family as well as the live-in servants necessary to support the family's needs. The quality of this design reflects the army's new acceptance of families within the military community.

The Golden Gate Bridge

Newly built highways wind across the Fort Baker hills toward the Golden Gate Bridge, 1938.

In 1933, construction began on the Golden Gate Bridge, the northern end of which would be anchored at Lime Point in Fort Baker. Some in the War Department initially had serious misgivings about the new bridge; not only would it rest on army land in San Francisco and Marin, there were unfounded fears the bridge might be brought down by enemy bombers or naval gunfire and block the harbor entrance.

Negotiations went on for several years between the army and the Golden Gate Bridge and Highway District, formed in 1928 by state legislation to design, construct, finance, and operate the bridge. Eventually, the parties agreed that in return for allowing the bridge to be built, any dis-

placed military installations (such as fortifications and support structures) would be rebuilt by the district. Also, US government and military personnel would be allowed to cross the bridge free of charge. (The latter stipulation was amended to allow only government vehicles "on official business" to cross free.) Finally, any temporary structures erected in conjunction with bridge construction would be removed from military property once the span was complete.

Two major structural bridge elements were planned at Fort Baker: the anchor block, where the bridge's two main cables would be secured on the Marin side, and the north tower of the bridge itself, to be located at the tip of Lime Point, almost (but not

quite) on top of the Coast Guard light station already occupying that spot.

Hundreds of bridge workers descended on the fort's shoreline as they made their way to the construction site. The west side of Horseshoe Cove was a scene of controlled chaos during the bridge's construction. A vast lay-down yard was created near the old Engineer Camp, in which huge girders and prefabricated car deck and tower sections were stockpiled. Closer to the Fort Baker parade, a giant concrete "batching plant" arose to manufacture concrete for the bridge's footings and anchor block. A small village of construction shops and offices sprang up along the fringes of the work site.

When the Golden Gate Bridge was finally completed, the north end of the bridge was the setting for the formal dedication ceremony, which took place there on May 28, 1937. Assembled dignitaries removed the four symbolic barricades that blocked the way to the new bridge: a chain of steel, another of gold, a third made of copper, and a California redwood log. Cutting torches removed the first three, while loggers bucked through the redwood log. Once removed, the Marin end of the bridge was officially opened.

The bridge district lived up to its promise, restoring the Fort Baker shoreline where the lay-down yard and concrete plant had once stood. The district also spent $575,000 building replacement facilities for the army at Fort Baker and the Presidio.

When completed, the Golden Gate Bridge was an engineering marvel. At the time, it was the longest single-span suspension bridge in the world, and the construction of its south tower in open-ocean conditions had been considered impossible. Today, the bridge has become an international icon and, for much of the world, the exemplification of San Francisco.

Although the Golden Gate Bridge's length and other dimensions have been exceeded by more modern bridges, its setting remains awe-inspiring and its statistics still have the power to stagger the imagination.

Facts and Figures

•Total length: 1.7 miles.

•Length of suspension span between towers: 4,200 feet.

•Height of towers: 746 feet.

•Rivets in each tower: approximately 1,200,000.

•Length of each main cable: 7,659 feet.

•Clearance above water at mid-span: 220 feet.

•Total weight of concrete anchorage block at Fort Baker: 60,000 tons.

•Total original weight of bridge and approaches: 894,500 tons.

•Original cost: $35 million.

•The two cables contain enough steel wire to circle the earth three times.

•The car deck can move 16 feet up and down, and sway 27 feet side to side.

•When first opened, a round-trip auto toll was $1 (more than $14 in today's dollars).

•The bridge's color is officially known as "International Orange."

•Original bridge workers were required to wear hard hats, a first in the 1930s.

•Eleven workers died during construction of the bridge, ten of them in one accident.

•Today, a crew of 45 painters and iron workers continues to maintain the bridge.

•The Golden Gate Bridge, Highway and Transportation District estimates it would cost about $1.4 billion to build another Golden Gate Bridge.

Golden Gate Bridge construction at Fort Baker, 1935. Left to right: north tower, Lime Point Coast Guard Station, access road, anchor block for the bridge cables, and concrete plant for anchorages and roadways.

Firing the Big Guns

The main reason for Fort Baker's existence was the defense of San Francisco Bay. At regular intervals, soldiers held target practice with the large-caliber artillery pieces that dotted the Marin and Presidio hills. Sometimes, the target practice took local citizens by surprise.

GREAT GUNS MAKE CITY PEOPLE GASP

The firing of the great 12-inch barbette guns from Fort Baker yesterday morning made all San Francisco sit up and listen. Seven shots were fired—and they were all full service charges, each one weighing 1,046 pounds.

The experiments were interrupted soon after noon by a heavy fog that settled down off the Golden Gate and hid the targets that were stationed 6,000 yards off the shore.

—*San Francisco Call,* May 27, 1910

In 1907, local Italian and Greek fishermen who had refused to leave the target zone outside the Golden Gate—the fishing was good—completely disrupted the army's carefully planned target practice:

When men and officers assembled at the various batteries at 10 o'clock yesterday morning they looked seaward and saw not only the targets

Fort Baker's gun batteries were manned by crews of young artillerymen who performed the physical tasks of moving ammunition, aiming the guns and calculating ranges to targets. At the moment of firing, unsuspecting crewmen could be knocked off their feet by the concussion of the large guns.

they were to annihilate, but a flock of fishing boats that humanity and international courtesy prevented them from annihilating. They gave it up at 1 o'clock and it is only because they are well disciplined men with tempers under control that Pietro and Nicholas and other swarthy ones who brave the dangers of the sea dropped safely into the basin at Fisherman's wharf last night.

— *San Francisco Call*, November 21, 1907

Eventually, the army started posting notices in local newspapers to alert merchant ships and fishing boats about upcoming target practices, and warned them to stay out of the target areas. Homeowners were advised to open their windows and remove fragile objects from shelves to prevent damage.

There were also some unforeseen results. According to dairy ranchers living near Fort Baker, cows would stop giving milk for several days following each target practice.

SHOT RECORD OF WORLD IS BROKEN

At Battery Spencer, soldiers not only fired the 12-inch guns, they also indulged in occasional bouts of horseplay.

Fort Baker Artillerymen Hit Target 4 Out of 6 Times at 10,000 Yards

Battery Spencer at Fort Baker, the highest 12 inch rifle battery in the world, established the world's record last Thursday. The remarkable record of four hits out of, six shots on a target 30 by 60 feet 10,000 yards distant was made by the Sixty-first company, Coast Artillery Corps, under the command of Lieutenant Halstead P. Councilman. But for the fact that the tow line was shot away, causing the target to drift, it is thought that six hits would have been made, as each gunner fired a shot before the fact was discovered.

— *San Francisco Call*, October 16, 1910

Chapter 5
World War II—The Fort Comes Alive: 1937 to 1945

Just as the Golden Gate Bridge was nearing completion, the army was shaking off the lassitude of the Depression and beginning to develop plans to upgrade its aging defenses of San Francisco Bay. Since 1905, only one modern long-range gun battery had been built in the bay's chain of fortifications, while advances in military technology had made most of the existing defenses obsolete. Many of the once daunting coastal weapons could now be handily outranged by larger and more accurate battleship guns, and the advent of aircraft and precision bombing had left many of the exposed gun emplacements vulnerable to aerial attack.

Plans were drawn up to construct new bombproof emplacements at several forts around the bay. But Fort Baker would get another technological improvement. Instead of attempting to modernize the fort's gun emplacements, which were both obsolescent and located too far inside the bay to have tactical value, military planners decided to convert Horseshoe Cove into a protected harbor for the small fleet of army boats that set out underwater minefields during wartime.

As the technology for controlled minefields improved, new

Coast Artillery soldiers preparing to drop a globe-shaped mine and its anchor into one of the minefields outside the Golden Gate.

defense strategies dictated that they be planted far outside the Golden Gate to stop an enemy fleet before it reached the bay itself. Oceangoing "mine planter" ships that could carry dozens of mines miles out to sea and drop them in place were constructed. As each electric mine was released, the planter also dropped a complicated array of electrical cables, anchors and floats. Smaller craft darted between the planter and the mines, helping position the mines in a carefully surveyed pattern and setting out their anchors and cabling.

By the 1930s, the army was looking for a new location for its mine depot and settled on Horseshoe Cove at Fort Baker as the ideal location. Its shoreline could easily handle the mine-storage buildings, docks, repair facilities and other shore-side structures integral to a mine depot, while underground ammunition rooms tunneled into Fort Baker's hills would provide storage for tons of TNT.

The first element of the Fort Baker Mine Depot was a mine-loading wharf completed in 1937 on the west side of Horseshoe Cove. A construction lull of several years followed, but in 1941, work resumed during the military build-up prior to America's entry into World War II. That year, the rest of the new mine depot was completed. New buildings included a spacious mine warehouse, a cable tank building

Forts Under the Bay

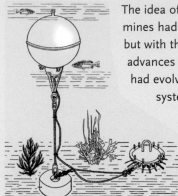

The idea of underwater, or "submarine," mines had been around since the Civil War, but with the tremendous technological advances that began in the 1890s, mines had evolved into a major defensive system. Twentieth-century underwater mines were generally buoyant devices, shaped like cylinders or globes and filled with several hundred pounds of dynamite, securely anchored to the bottom. A spiderweb of waterproof electrical cables connected the mines to an underground shore-side control room called a "mine casemate," from which they could be set off either individually or in groups. Artillery spotters watched the minefields and relayed enemy ship positions to the underground casemate, letting the operators know when a ship was passing over a group of mines. Then, an electric switch was thrown and the mines exploded directly beneath the ship. The resulting explosion and water pressure could crush a ship's hull like an eggshell.

Underwater minefields were complex weapons systems that required constant maintenance. They couldn't be left in place for extended periods, since the continual pounding of waves and the corrosive effects of salt water on steel and rubber would eventually render them useless. Instead, the army's defense plans called for the mines to be "planted" only in time of war or threat of war. Until then, the mines and their miles of cabling and associated control equipment were stored in shore-side mine depots. For safety, the TNT fillings were removed during storage.

The simplified diagram shows the three overlapping minefields that protected the entrance to San Francisco Bay during World War II.

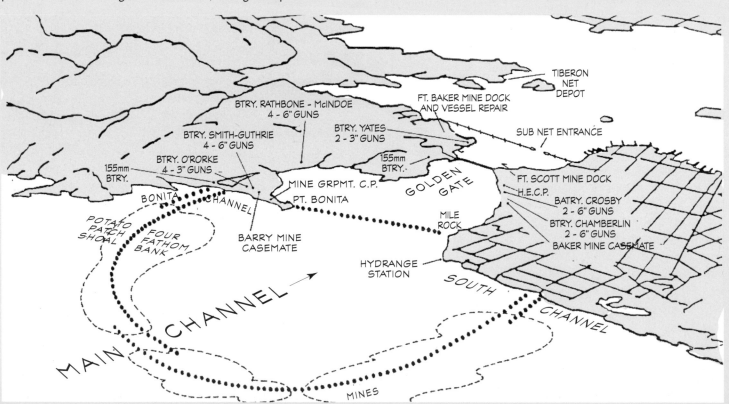

A small fleet of vessels, nicknamed "the army's navy," stood ready to load the mines, plant them in the ocean, and stretch the electrical cabling between the individual mines and from the mine groups to shore. Even during peacetime, these vessels had to be ready on short notice. As a result, mine depots usually included loading piers for mine planters, boat slips for smaller craft and shore-side repair shops.

Coast Artillery troops regularly practiced planting and retrieving small groups of mines, but the mine fields of San Francisco Bay had only been entirely planted once, during the Spanish-American War of 1898, and then from a mine depot located on Yerba Buena Island (beneath today's San Francisco–Oakland Bay Bridge). These early minefields stretched in an arc from the San Francisco waterfront to Alcatraz Island, and from Alcatraz to Angel Island and the Marin shore—well within the sheltered waters of the bay.

Although underwater minefields might logically seem to be naval weapons, they were actually placed under control of the Coast Artillery as an integral part of the defense of the country's harbor and river mouths.

The Ellery W. Niles *(below) was described as "the last word in mine planters" and the most beautiful ship the army ever built. Launched in 1937, she was stationed at Fort Baker throughout World War II. Following her wartime service, she became a Signal Corps cable laying ship and a civilian research vessel. She was scuttled in 1985 and is now a popular dive attraction off Key West, Florida, known by her last name, the* Cayman Salvage Master *(right).*

for storing reels of underwater cable, two underground loading rooms near the wharf where TNT would be placed in the mines, explosives magazines and an underground power plant. A stone jetty projecting into the cove created a sheltered boat basin for the small craft that were part of the mine-planting operation.

The rest of Fort Baker also experienced a rebirth during the pre-war mobilization. The United States had initiated a draft in 1940 to induct young men into the armed forces, and in 1941, the newly trained soldiers began to arrive at the harbor defense forts. These young men, who self-deprecatingly called themselves "GIs" for "Government Issued," manned the existing Coast Artillery fortifications around the bay and helped construct yet more defenses, such as anti-aircraft emplacements, searchlight positions and super-secret radar

The interior of a mine storehouse, like this one at Fort Scott, contained racks of empty mines, cables, tools and anchors for holding down the buoyant mines.

installations. By the time the United States entered World War II, the troops assigned to the Harbor Defenses of San Francisco (HDSF for short) numbered in the thousands.

News of the Japanese attack on Pearl Harbor reached San Francisco late in the morning of December 7, 1941. Immediately, announcements went out over the radio ordering military personnel to return to their posts. The commanding general at Fort Scott put all the fortifications on immediate alert, and soldiers poured out of their barracks and moved into batteries, trenches, dugouts and observation posts. By noon, all elements of the HDSF were fully manned.

At Fort Baker, the mine depot went into action, and the small fleet of army boats began laying underwater minefields. This was no practice drill; there was a real fear of attack, and the harbor defenses were on full alert. According to official HDSF history, all three minefields were active by December 8. The fears weren't unfounded. Japanese submarines sank several merchant ships along the West Coast during December 1941, and postwar research revealed that one Japanese plan contemplated using a submarine to shell San Francisco on Christmas Eve.

At Fort Baker, where most of the Endicott batteries had been stripped of their big guns during the World War I, new defense activities focused on emplacing anti-aircraft guns on the hilltops and rapid-fire guns along the shore at Horseshoe

Mines had be brought up periodically for cleaning and repair. In this 1942 view, a cylindrical mine shows an impressive amount of marine growth accumulated during its underwater service.

High Explosives and Cracked Crab

The war had a devastating effect on San Francisco's crab industry when, in February 1942, regulations went into effect banning potential "enemy aliens" from the San Francisco waterfront. This included the Fisherman's Wharf area and its colorful flotilla of crab boats, which were manned almost exclusively by Italian fishermen. San Francisco's famous crab fleet vanished virtually overnight.

Lieutenant Colonel Felix Usis, a dedicated lover of the local Dungeness crab and officer in charge of the mine fleet at Fort Baker, decided to take matters into his own hands. Or

Lieutenant Colonel Felix Usis

rather, he decided to take matters into the army's hands. Usis put the HDSF Mine Flotilla to work as a crabbing fleet, equipping the smaller boats with crab pots. When the boats set out each day to maintain the minefields, they planted crab pots along the way. At day's end, the soldiers recovered the pots and their clawed contents and returned to Fort Baker. Usis' crabbers were soon furnishing fresh crab to officers' messes throughout the Harbor Defenses.

Some of the army cooks were unfamiliar with how to prepare crabs, however. One cook was observed standing next to a pot full of live crabs,

Forklift carrying a "ground" mine at the Fort Baker Depot, circa 1946. Unlike buoyant mines, ground mines rested on the bottom of the ocean.

whacking them with a stick as they attempted to crawl out. Seems the cook had filled the pot with cold water, turned on the burner and immediately dropped in the crabs. No one had told him the proper method was to dunk the crabs into already boiling water.

View of Horseshoe Cove from the nearly complete Mine Wharf. The quartermaster complex and corrals are visible in the distance.

Opposite, top: Work began in 1937 on a new Mine Depot at Fort Baker that would handle the storage, loading and maintenance of the Main Channel and North Channel minefields.

Opposite, bottom: The new Fort Baker Station Hospital, December 1941.

Cove and Kirby Cove (old Gravelly Beach) to guard against swift torpedo boats. The army also began construction of a sprawling hospital along the northern edge of Horseshoe Cove. The 229-bed Fort Baker Station Hospital was designed specifically to handle the medical needs of HDSF soldiers as well as to take some of the patient load off the Presidio's Letterman General Hospital. A network of covered ramps and walkways connected the maze of single-story, wood-frame wards, allowing recovering soldiers using crutches or wheelchairs to move comfortably around the facility.

Navy sailors and Coast Artillery soldiers worked together to learn the art of splicing cables at the Fort Baker mine depot.

Soldiers of the 54th Coast Artillery regiment at a camouflaged 155mm gun emplacement hastily erected at Kirby Cove after the Pearl Harbor attack.

As the war progressed, the Station Hospital increasingly handled overflow patients from Letterman, many of them casualties from the Pacific island battlefields. The Red Cross, USO and Armed Forces Entertainment Committee brought movies and other diversions to the recovering men.

But it was the mine depot—designated Mine Command Headquarters—that performed the major part of Fort Baker's wartime duties. By 1945, the waters outside the Golden Gate were laced with 481 submerged mines.

To augment the busy depot's operations, in 1943, a boat repair facility was built on the east side of the cove. Providing critical maintenance for the mine fleet, the repair facility included a fuel dock, a fifty-ton crane, two marine railways, machine shops, and carpentry and paint shops. To protect the new facility from wave action, another stone jetty, the Satterlee Breakwater, was constructed across Horseshoe Cove, this time from its eastern shore. The eastern face of Point Cavallo behind Battery Yates was quarried for rock to build the breakwater.

Wartime expansion wasn't limited just to Horseshoe Cove. As more and more troops arrived to operate the mine depot, hospital, repair shops and defense installations, dozens of temporary buildings appeared in various corners of the fort. Some structures, like barracks and storehouses, were located within the original 1905 Fort Baker cantonment, even on the parade ground. Many others went up on the west side of the Baker-Barry Tunnel, where a sub-post called (logically) West Portal was established. Other temporary structures brought the total number of buildings in Fort Baker to 159 by mid-December 1942.

The wartime changes at the fort also resulted in substantial filling along the Horseshoe Cove bayfront that would never take place today without extensive environmental reviews. The pre-war shoreline had remained remarkably unchanged from the time the Spanish had first anchored there in the eighteenth century. But between 1941 and 1944, the original sandy beach disappeared during construction of the Station Hospital, destroyed when a sturdy bulkhead was built along the shore's edge to provide level ground for the new medical complex and the army's marine repair shops. The two stone jetties and marine railways projecting into the little bay further erased the shoreline. By war's end, Horseshoe Cove had little resemblance to its original appearance.

New armament for Fort Barry being unloaded at the Fort Baker pier, June 1939.

The end of World War II in August 1945 marked Fort Baker's demise as a harbor defense fort. In the immediate post-war years, Fort Baker began losing its claws. The mobile anti-aircraft and anti-torpedo-boat guns were packed up and towed away for storage, and the last pair of Endicott weapons (still mounted at Battery Yates) was cut up for scrap in its emplacement. The navy's submarine net stretching from San Francisco to Sausalito was removed and the mines anchored outside the gate were hauled up from the bottom.

Three years later, an army clerk penned an ungrammatical entry in the fort's record book, documenting the end of its defensive history: "2 Nov 1948. There is no fixed or movable arament [sic] at Fort Baker."

The post was about to embark on the last role of its military life: as an administrative and logistics center.

The Fort Baker Waterfront

Seen from Horseshoe Cove, the San Francisco skyline glitters in the distance. Nearby is the stone jetty where Coast Guard rescue vessels are moored, and to its west is the road that leads out toward the old Mine Wharf, Lime Point and the Golden Gate Bridge. The Travis Sailing Center, with its repair shops and boat slips, is located on the west side of the cove. Overlooking the sailing center is the concrete monolith of Battery Yates, one of Fort Baker's coastal defense fortifications. Here are a few of its contemporary attractions.

THE FORT BAKER MINE DEPOT

The Fort Baker mine depot buildings are spread along the west side of Horseshoe Cove. The most prominent structures are the above-ground mine storehouse and cable tank building (Building 407, below) where unloaded mines and miles of underwater cable were stored during peace time. The other major feature is the mine wharf, where army vessels tied up when loading mines and cables.

The most hazardous activity at any mine depot was the storage and handling of high explosives, and many of the Fort Baker mine depot buildings reflect the dangerous aspects of the job. To avoid accidental explosions, a series of underground buildings were tunneled into the bluffs on the west side of the cove to protect them from enemy attack. Their interior rooms remained cool and dark, important when storing high explosives.

Building 412, closest to the Mine Wharf, housed the mine-loading rooms. In these dark concrete chambers, soldiers carefully poured TNT into the mines just before they were placed aboard the mine-planting ships. Small quantities of TNT were stored in Building 411. A close look at Building 410, which was used as the detonator magazine, reveals the "Explosives" and "No Smoking" signs. Building 409 housed a power plant that provided electricity to the entire mine depot.

The army built two stone breakwaters to protect the cove from the waves and wakes of passing ships. Here, small boats assigned to the mine fleet could be safely anchored. On the far side of the cove, the army also built a repair facility where boats could be hauled out of the water for maintenance. Today, the repair facility is used by pleasure craft moored at Horseshoe Cove.

Opposite: Comparison views of Horseshoe Cove, circa 1912 and 2011, taken a century apart. All of the original shoreline has disappeared under rock fill excavated from nearby hillsides, and even the tip of Point Cavallo has been shaved off for wartime use. The only unchanged feature is Battery Yates, overlooking the present-day yacht harbor.

COAST GUARD STATION GOLDEN GATE

The picket-enclosed compound is the administrative and barracks complex for Coast Guard personnel assigned to Station Golden Gate. These men and women, members of Homeland Security, are on continuous standby and ready to assist vessels in distress or carry out law-enforcement actions. The boats used by the Coast Guard are tied up along the breakwater across from the underground mine depot magazines. These powerful, self-righting watercraft are capable of handling the roughest sea conditions imaginable, and can even turn completely over and come back up for more.

The original Coast Guard station was sited on the opposite side of the Golden Gate in the Presidio of San Francisco. Changing technology made the old station obsolete and, in 1990, a new complex was built here on shore of Horseshoe Cove. Although of contemporary vintage, the building's architecture carefully complements the historic design of the 1905 army buildings lining the parade ground behind the station.

NATURE AT HORSESHOE COVE

The open water of Horseshoe Cove—which also contains eel grass, considered a special aquatic resource because of its rarity and the high-quality habitat it provides—supports a great variety of fish, bird and mammal species. Located within a designated critical habitat area for the winter run of Sacramento River Chinook salmon, it is part of the Dungeness crab migratory corridor between the Farallon Islands and San Francisco Bay. The cove and the bay waters adjacent to Fort Baker are among the most important spawning areas on the Pacific Coast for Pacific herring, and cormorants, gulls, endangered California brown pelicans, western grebes, sea lions and harbor seals are also frequent visitors.

Nearby ridgetops provide one of the last remaining habitats for the endangered mission blue butterfly *(Icaricia icarioides missionensis)*. Squeezed by urban growth, this federally listed endangered species only exists in a few scattered areas on the San Francisco Peninsula and in the Marin Headlands, including Fort Baker. The butterflies lay their eggs on several species of low-growing lupine plants. Here, the eggs hatch to become caterpillars, then lie dormant in the grasslands for more than half the year before forming pupae and then emerging in April as adult butterflies. Their adult lifespan is extremely short: three to ten days. Most mission blues never venture more than 2,000 feet (600 meters) from their home lupine patch.

Among the threats to the mission blue are off-road vehicles and off-trail foot traffic, which can kill or crush the caterpillars or their lupine host plants. To help protect this endangered species, some areas of Fort Baker are closed to hiking.

BATTERY YATES

Completed in 1905, Battery Yates' six "rapid-firing" guns were positioned to defend against enemy vessels coming through the Golden Gate. Unlike the larger-caliber guns mounted elsewhere at Fort Baker, these small guns could focus their fire on fast-moving and lightly armored craft such as destroyers or torpedo boats.

The small size and light weight of the projectiles (only 15 pounds) resulted in extremely fast rates of fire, sometimes up to 30 shots per minute. However, shooting into the often-crowded waters of San Francisco Bay could be hazardous to civilian vessels. As a result, Battery Yates' guns were only fired a few times in target practice.

The battery is built on two levels. The six 3-inch caliber guns were mounted on the upper story, while ammunition storage magazines occupied the lower level. Taking the stairs, soldiers hand-carried the 15-pound shells to the guns. Additional rooms (fitted with barred windows) served as storage rooms and offices.

The army considered Yates to be obsolete by World War II. After spending the war protecting the antisubmarine net at the entrance to the bay, its guns were scrapped in 1946.

Two aerial views of the post-war fort show the development of Horseshoe Cove at its height, circa 1960. In the view above, the Mine Wharf and Satterlee Breakwater stretch out from opposite sides of the cove. The arrival of color photography (facing page, circa 1970) revealed the color scheme of the Station Hospital and boat repair complex: cream colored buildings with red roofs.

Chapter 6
Cold War and Base Closure: 1946–1999

Shortly after the end of World War II, the army's three mine planters began the laborious task of clearing the three minefields outside the Golden Gate and recovering the miles of associated cabling stretched along the ocean bottom. Back at the Fort Baker depot, soldiers carefully removed the mines' TNT fillings, sandblasted the barnacles and rust off their empty steel casings, repainted the now-inert weapons, and placed them in storage in the mine storehouse. Underwater cables were wound back onto their reels and dropped into the flooded storage pools in the cable tank building to await the day they were again needed to protect the harbor.

Just as the rise of ironclad ships and long-range artillery during the Civil War had made hulking masonry forts obsolete, the advent of long-range bombers and nuclear weapons revealed the weaknesses of America's coastal defenses. Huge artillery guns and underwater mines, meant to counter battleships and invasion fleets, were useless against multi-engine bombers flying tens of thousands of feet overhead. The threat of warships attacking American harbors was gone, replaced by the knowledge that a single airplane carrying a thermonuclear device could destroy an entire city. Increasingly, the military began researching the use of radar-directed anti-aircraft guns and missiles to counter the threat of high-altitude bombers.

Fort Baker and the rest of the harbor defenses—and indeed, the entire Coast Artillery Corps—quickly became outmoded. Immediately after the war's end, the army began disarming its coastal defense batteries and cutting up the weapons for salvage.

The army's responsibility for maintaining the minefields of the nation's ports lasted only slightly longer, coming to an inglorious end in 1949 when it was stripped of its underwater-defense role. The final blow to the Coast Artillery Corps came late that year, when the Department of Defense announced that responsibility for controlled submarine mines would be transferred from the army to the navy. From that point on, the western portion of Horseshoe Cove, with its mine buildings and magazines and loading pier, came under the navy's jurisdiction. The navy's tenancy at the cove would last ten more years; as late as April 1959, Fort Baker's roster of active military activities still included "navy mine-laying operations."

The Coast Artillery Corps itself was officially disbanded in 1950, but its role defending American harbors would shortly re-emerge as the army's new Anti-Aircraft Artillery (AAA) branch.

The Station Hospital adjacent to the mine depot also experienced a substantial slowdown in patients as the war wound down and the number of sick and wounded soldiers tapered off. The hospital was closed briefly in October 1946, only to reopen suddenly a few weeks later. The reason was decidedly non-military: it had been more than nine months since the first GIs from the Pacific and European Theaters had returned home, and the nation was experiencing the first wave of what came to be called the Baby Boom. According to

Nike-Hercules missiles at a launch site at Fort Barry, one of eleven Nike sites commanded from the Air Defense Artillery Headquarters at Fort Baker. This launch site is preserved today as part of the Golden Gate National Recreation Area.

army personnel who served at the Station Hospital, it was converted into a 100-bed facility that primarily served as a giant maternity ward for military dependents.

From 1946 to 1954, the fort functioned primarily as a residential area for staff assigned to the Presidio of San Francisco on the far side of the bridge. Many temporary barracks buildings at West Portal and elsewhere were boarded up or converted to residences for married enlisted personnel. With the mine depot under navy control (but relatively inactive), the busiest parts of the post were the army's boat repair facility and the old Station Hospital, which eventually assumed the role of an army laboratory and research center.

Though the minefields were transferred to navy oversight, the east side of Horseshoe Bay remained under jurisdiction of the army, which continued to use the Marine Repair Facility to maintain its extensive collection of harbor craft. Together with the rest of Fort Baker, the boat shops and hospital became a sub-post of the Presidio of San Francisco. The fort no longer even had a commanding officer. Instead, the post commander of the Presidio of San Francisco served as Fort Baker's "landlord," overseeing the various military activities that took place within its buildings and cove.

Following World War II, Fort Baker hosted an impressive array of functions, among them, a 6th Army laboratory; a regional Air Defense Command headquarters; a reserve and training center; a recruiting command; a US Corps of Engineers' port construction unit; and housing for army personnel assigned to these commands as well as to the 6th Army, which was headquartered at the Presidio and Letterman General Hospital. In many ways, Fort Baker became a bedroom community for the Presidio.

The outbreak of the Korean War in 1950 brought about a new round of activity. As defense against attack by Soviet aircraft, the army rapidly installed radar-directed 90mm and 120mm anti-aircraft guns at strategic points around the perimeter of San Francisco Bay. Although none of the guns was physically located at Fort Baker, there were batteries nearby in the Presidio, Fort Barry and Fort Cronkhite. Other anti-aircraft batteries protected air force bases around the state. In 1951, the army designated Fort Baker as headquarters for the Western Army Anti-Aircraft Command. Shortly after, on March 10, 1952, the headquarters of the 47th Anti-Aircraft Artillery (AAA) Brigade arrived at the fort as the parent organization for all anti-aircraft units in eight western states. The brigade's headquarters were located in the former artillery barracks facing the parade ground.

Just as the old Coast Artillery guns had become outmoded by advances in air power, the AAA guns rapidly became obsolete as newer long-range bombers came into production, aircraft that could fly higher than any gun could fire. In response, in 1954, the army began to replace the fixed anti-aircraft guns with radar-directed guided missiles fired from either mobile or fixed batteries. These were the famous Nike-Ajax of the Cold War, capable of bringing down an enemy bomber at ranges of 30 miles or more. The 47th AAA Brigade assumed command of the Nike units as they came online in the mid-1950s.

One of the eleven missile sites constructed by the army to protect San Francisco Bay was located on Angel Island, sever-al miles from Fort Baker. In order to supply this isolated site, the army's engineers constructed a new ferry pier at Horseshoe Cove near the repair facility. This pier served the motor launch that carried military personnel and their families to and from the island. (Today, Angel Island is a state park, but its link to Fort Baker continues. A motorized barge shuttles daily between the island and Fort Baker, carrying vehicles and other oversize equipment.)

By the late 1950s, the 6th Army's need for the boat repair facility began to dwindle, and some time around 1960, the army transferred the main shop building to the Presidio Yacht Club, which had been established in May 1959 to provide recreational opportunities for active-duty military personnel and retirees. The club was given permission to use the building and its shops and marine railways, and to construct private boat slips near Satterlee Breakwater. Club members eventually converted portions of the shop building into a cozy wood-paneled lounge complete with a bar, dance floor and tables. Windows on the south side framed stunning views of the Golden Gate Bridge.

The Anti-Aircraft Artillery was renamed the US Army Air Defense Command (ARADCOM) in the late 1950s, but the change had little practical effect on Fort Baker, which remained the command headquarters for air defense of the western states. Within ARADCOM, there were further command responsibilities and reorganizations, and the 47th AAA Brigade evolved into the 6th Region, US Army Air Defense Command, which included the Los Angeles,

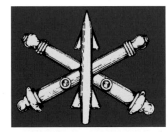

The insignia of the army's new Air Defense Artillery combined the antique cannon of the artillery branch with a modern supersonic missile.

San Francisco and Seattle defensive areas. The 6th Region headquarters continued to occupy the Fort Baker barracks until the army phased out the Nike missile defense system in 1974.

Much of the open land around the bay was owned by the Department of Defense. Then, during the 1950s and '60s, the army—once considered a stable component of the Bay Area's economy—started moving people and jobs to southern California. Since these bases were no longer needed, the military began to sell much of its prime surplus real estate to the highest bidder. Bay Area residents were concerned about plans for large-scale commercial and housing developments; in San Francisco, construction proposals at the Presidio and Fort Miley, both picturesque coastal lands, also prompted environmental outcries.

Bay Area citizens and local agencies, outraged at the prospect of losing beautiful and much-loved open space, considered alternatives to the various development proposals.

More than sixty individual organizations banded together, forming a single advocacy group: People for a Golden Gate National Recreation Area. Together with the San Francisco Planning and Urban Renewal Agency, the San Francisco Recreation and Park Department and Congressman Phillip

For many years, the 561st Port Construction Engineer Company was a highly visible tenant of Fort Baker. Their duties ranged from building and repairing harbor facilities to training as combat soldiers (opposite, bottom).

Burton, they began to ask the question: Could this land could be set aside, protected for everyone's enjoyment?

At the time, both Democrats and Republicans were interested in conserving open space, and Congressman Burton was able to push through a bill calling for the inclusion of surplus military land and adjacent non-military open space in a new type of urban national park. President Richard Nixon, who was up for re-election, flew to San Francisco to see the landscape for himself. After taking a well-publicized tour of the proposed park, Nixon endorsed the bill, and on October 27, 1972, signed "An Act to Establish the Golden Gate National Recreation Area" (Public Law 92-589).

Golden Gate National Recreation Area (GGNRA) was intended to protect these and other lands surrounding San Francisco Bay for future generations by placing them under control of the National Park Service. The newly authorized park included ranch lands, existing state and urban park parcels, and the abandoned federal penitentiary on Alcatraz,

site of the much-publicized nineteen-month occupation by Native American activists. (The Alcatraz Occupation and the controversy surrounding the island's future had, in fact, been one of the catalysts that led to the creation of the sprawling new park.)

The army, which recognized the historic significance of Fort Baker, assisted historians in nominating the post to the National Register of Historic Places. Originally put forward because of its long legacy of coastal fortifications, the post's exceptionally well-preserved examples of turn-of-the-century military architecture surrounding the main parade were also eventually recognized to have significance. Fort Baker, together with Forts Barry and Cronkhite, was added to the National Register in 1973.

At the time GGNRA was created, the most extensive open lands were still under the control of the army: Forts Baker, Barry and Cronkhite in Marin County and Forts Mason and Miley and the historic Presidio in San Francisco. Under

The abandoned fortifications of Fort Baker symbolized the posts' decreasing defensive role during the Cold War. Sometimes, though, the army found new uses for the old batteries as training sites.

terms of Congressman Burton's bill, these tracts of land would be transferred from the Department of Defense to the National Park Service as their military missions ended. It took more than thirty years, but eventually all of these former military posts became part of GGNRA.

The military lands within the Marin Headlands began to be transferred to the National Park Service in 1974 when the last of the Nike missile sites was shut down. The open space and abandoned fortifications were transferred first, followed by excess military warehouses, barracks and residential

buildings. By the late 1980s, the only sizable area under military control was Fort Baker's cantonment and boat harbor. Here, the historic Coast Artillery post with its charming 1900s-era homes was occupied by military personnel assigned to Letterman General Hospital and the 6th Army at the Presidio. Along the shoreline at Horseshoe Cove, the Presidio Yacht Club continued to serve the recreational needs of active duty and retired military. The NPS and the army expected this partnership to last for many more years.

However, Fort Baker's future changed forever in 1990 with

the Base Realignment and Closure Act (BRAC), promulgated by Congress as a nationwide cost-cutting program to reduce military installations. Among the bases on the BRAC list was the Presidio of San Francisco. With the Presidio slated to close, and with it, 6th Army headquarters and Letterman Hospital, it was only a matter of time before Fort Baker would also become redundant. At that point, under the terms of the legislation that created GGNRA, the National Park Service would assume ownership of the Presidio and its sub-post at Fort Baker.

The actual transfer of the Presidio of San Francisco to the NPS took place on October 1, 1994, complete with elaborate ceremonies on the Presidio's main parade ground. The Presidio, the longest-serving army post in the United States, traced its history back to the original Spanish military outpost established in 1776. It was an emotional ceremony for many old soldiers and their families.

Closing down extensive military commands such as the 6th Army and Letterman isn't a quick operation, however, and it took several years for the numbers of troops to actually drop. At Fort Baker, military medical families continued to live in the officers' quarters facing the parade ground until 1997, when Letterman Hospital finally closed.

Despite the dramatic 1994 base transfer ceremonies at the Presidio, the true end of the US Army's role in protecting San Francisco came on October 30, 2002, when the formal transfer of Fort Baker took place. The army was represented by officers and a color guard from Travis Air Force Base, California (the last military presence at Fort Baker), while the National Park Service was represented by rangers in full dress uniform and General Superintendent Brian O'Neill. In a ceremony that marked the end of one era and the beginning of another, a color guard first lowered the United States flag to symbolize the base closure, and then immediately re-hoisted it to recognize the new "command": the National Park Service's Golden Gate National Recreation Area. It was time for the next chapter in the fort's history.

National Park Service and US Air Force personnel at the base transfer ceremony, October 30, 2002. The banners represented the units of the Golden Gate National Recreation Area.

Fort Baker's main post today, viewed from Vista Point near the Golden Gate Bridge. The restored 1905 buildings and parade ground are complemented by the contemporary Lodge buildings higher on the slopes.

Chapter 7
The Fort Reborn: 2002 to the Present

Planning for Fort Baker's future as part of a National Park Service site had begun long before the army departed. Every NPS unit has a General Management Plan (GMP), which lays out the site's long-term direction and use concepts. Fort Baker was included in GGNRA's 1980 GMP; at Fort Baker, habitat for the mission blue butterfly, a federally listed endangered species, would be protected and open space would be preserved. The historic army maintenance buildings were to be rehabilitated. For the main army cantonment, the plan envisioned an environmental study center and retreat facility that would use the former barracks and residences as classroom spaces and dormitories. Non-historic buildings would be torn down, enhancing the early-1900s appearance of the main post and maximizing recreational space and views of the bay.

One of the first non-military occupants of Fort Baker was the Bay Area Discovery Museum, a children's museum. The museum approached the National Park Service and proposed the site as a home for their new institution. Instead of constructing a new complex, the Discovery Museum proposed renovating seven historic army buildings that had originally served such workaday post uses as blacksmith shop, gas station, wagon shed and bakery, converting them into an educational play land of exhibits and workshops focusing on the natural wonders of San Francisco Bay.

The conversion of the buildings was carried out according to the Secretary of the Interior's Standards for Historic Preservation, the gold standard for rehabilitating our nation's historic resources—a set of guidelines ensuring that historic integrity is protected during renovation. The result of this conversion was a resounding success that continues to delight children (and their parents). The museum has won several preservation and design awards, including the prestigious National Historic Preservation Award from the President's Advisory Council on Historic Preservation.

Then, in the late 1990s, Golden Gate National Recreation Area and its nonprofit cooperating association, Golden Gate National Parks Conservancy (then known as Golden Gate National Park Association), began to write the Fort Baker Master Plan, an Environmental Impact Statement (EIS), and planning documents and business plans, and to conduct surveys of the post's existing infrastructure and buildings.

The reality of Fort Baker quickly became clear: while the century-old main post buildings were charming to look at, they presented a wide variety of structural challenges. Most of the porches were riddled with dry rot, and interiors were a maze of bad wiring, non-historic walls, asbestos insulation and lead-based paint. Built to century-old specifications and designed for occupancy by healthy young soldiers and their families, none of the historic buildings were up to seismic codes, nor were any accessible to those with disabilities. In order to accommodate modern uses, the buildings would have to be completely rehabilitated and would need full-time occupants who would take care of the old structures and bring new life and activities to them.

In 1999, the National Park Service released a "Request for Qualifications for the Retreat and Conference Center at Fort Baker." As laid out in the RFQ, the future retreat and conference center had four key goals:

1. Develop an excellent adaptive reuse and historic preservation project.

2. Incorporate sustainability in design, construction and operation, creating a "green" facility modeled on the industry's best practices.

3. Minimize impact on existing natural and cultural resources and the visitor experience.

4. Minimize automobile use associated with traffic to and within the site, including within adjacent communities.

Response to this request was spirited. In 2002, after an extensive competition process, the National Park Service selected Passport Resorts of San Francisco, who had partnered with Equity Community Builders to create the Fort Baker Retreat Group. Long-term lease in hand, the group proceeded to finance, carry out rehabilitation and operate the project.

A name was needed for the retreat and conference center, one that drew inspiration from the fort's setting as well as its military past. The final choice was Cavallo Point: The Lodge at the Golden Gate, a name that reflected the historic post's geographic location and also harkened back to its early Spanish and Mexican roots.

Using voluminous documentation on the post provided by the National Park Service, the partnership began to develop preservation plans for each of the historic buildings. One of the key principles was that while meeting the challenge of bringing the public buildings up to modern life (safety and disability access codes), as much of the historic character of the post as possible would be preserved. As with the earlier Bay Area Discovery Museum project, all planning was guided by the Secretary of the Interior's Standards for Historic Preservation.

The development team decided that the barracks and gym on the east side of the parade ground would be converted into public spaces, restaurant and lounge, and classroom and meeting spaces. The officer and NCO duplexes (some of which sported five bedrooms and servants' quarters) as well as the former post headquarters would be modified into smaller rooms and suites for overnight guests. The old post chapel, high on the slope above the rest of the cantonment, would be turned into an assembly and meeting space. In an apt match-up, the lodge's laundry and maintenance facility would occupy a cavernous warehouse that once held underwater mines.

One of the biggest challenges was to make the multistory enlisted soldiers' barracks fully accessible to disabled visitors. Originally, the multiple levels were connected with staircases, but with careful planning to ensure that few historic walls were moved, it was determined that elevators could be incorporated into the core of each building, fitted snugly within existing walls of what had been barber shops. On the barracks' exteriors, wheelchair ramps were subtly incorporated into the new front porches and the rehabilitated rear porches.

Work at the lodge began in late 2006 and continued for nearly two years. The statistics were impressive: rehabilitation of twenty-eight historic buildings, construction of fourteen contemporary buildings (thirteen new overnight-accommodation buildings and the Healing Arts Center and Spa) and new landscaping. The project also included small-scale details like sidewalks, street lamps, and resurfaced roads and parking areas. The National Park Service restored the post's historic parade ground to its 1930s configuration and reseeded the landscape with drought-resistant grass.

Cavallo Point: The Lodge at Golden Gate was officially opened in June 2008, and was immediately recognized as a benchmark example of historic site preservation, rehabilitation and sustainable design. Since the lodge's opening, it has not only won numerous awards, it has also become one of the nation's outstanding examples of public/private partnerships.

Nonetheless, the rebirth of Fort Baker is not complete. Future plans call for improvements along the Horseshoe Cove waterfront, upgraded trails, new interpretative signs and displays, and increased public amenities such as overlooks and picnic areas. Plans also call for the ongoing protection and enhancement of more than 40 acres of natural landscape surrounding the post, including additional acres of habitat for the mission blue butterfly.

A Green Lodge

The designers of Cavallo Point: The Lodge at the Golden Gate, honoring its unique location within a national park, incorporated numerous green building materials and techniques to minimize its carbon footprint. Among them:

- Photovoltaic panels that produce electricity sufficient to power the buildings.
- Blue-jean insulation in the contemporary buildings, as well as radiant heat and hot water provided by tankless water heaters.
- Low VOC (volatile organic compound) glues, paints and carpets.
- In new construction, floors and ceilings made from rapidly renewable materials, including bamboo, wool and cork.
- An innovative, on-site, recycled-water laundry facility that reuses 70 percent of its wash water.
- Natural gas rather than wood-burning stoves.
- Drought-tolerant California native plants grown in the park's nursery for landscaping around the new lodge.
- Minimal outdoor lighting to encourage wildlife inhabitation.

This effort has been celebrated with numerous awards, among them the prestigious LEED Gold Certification (2010), as well as the California State Preservation Foundation's Preservation Design Award (2008); the National Preservation Honor and Governor's Environment and Economic Leadership Awards (2009); and the first National Park Service "Designing the Parks" Award (2010).

Bringing Back the Fort

As part of the parade-ground rehabilitation, planners set up test plots with various types of drought-tolerant grasses.
(Notice the porchless barracks in the background in this 2006 photo.)

A key feature in transforming the historic fort into the modern lodge was the restoration of the original main parade ground. When the army occupied Fort Baker, the 13-acre parade functioned as both the physical and the organizational center of post life. In its pragmatic way, the army was less concerned about history than it was about accommodating the day-to-day needs of soldiers and their families. By the 1950s, the parade ground stopped being used for its original purpose and instead, became the site of a number of more ephemeral amenities, among them, a large asphalt parking lot; a long garage that once housed mobile searchlights; and a baseball diamond, backstop and bleachers. In order to return the parade to its historic configuration, the National Park Service designed

a new project that would restore it to its general appearance and characteristics circa the 1930s. In addition to removing the non-historic elements listed previously, the project was attentive to the visual and resource aspects of the parade itself. The eucalyptus trees that once lined Murray Circle, which rings the parade ground, were removed, and new trees were planted to recreate the historic pattern, which was determined by study of historic maps, drawings and photographs. The new trees—including spotted gum (*Eucalyptus maculata*) and water gum (*Tristaniopsis laurina*)—were selected because their shape and growth pattern matched those of the original trees; they should eventually grow to about 35 feet. To restore the verdant appearance of the

parade, a grass known as Aurora Gold Fescue was chosen for its slow growth, good performance, and low water and maintenance needs. In the summer and fall, this grass goes dormant and turns a golden color, then greens up again with the winter rains.

An irrigation system connected to an on-site weather station was installed to maintain the new grass and trees until they can grow without additional water. And sharp-eyed visitors will notice that new concrete sidewalks and curbs match the historic concrete work found in other areas of the post.

Barracks Porch Restoration

The wood-frame barracks constructed in 1902 to house more than one hundred Coast Artillery soldiers were built from standard army plans, which included wide, two-story front porches as elegant architectural elements. In the 1950s, probably due to maintenance issues, the army removed the original porches, which diminished the integrity and significance of the barracks as well as their overall appearance. The rehabilitation plan called for converting these barracks buildings into assembly, dining and office spaces.

The National Park Service does not usually restore missing architectural elements unless there is sufficient historic documentation to justify it. But when the historic preservation professionals discovered the original 1902 building plans as well as several historical photographs of the barracks, the decision was made to reconstruct the missing porches. New construction materials were used, so that in the future, architects and historians will be able to differentiate between the original 1902 porches and the replacements added a century later.

Pressed-Metal Ceilings Return to Their Original Glory

Decorative pressed-metal ceilings can be found in most of the Fort Baker buildings, including the barracks, officers' housing, the post headquarters, even the guard house. The intricate designs of the metal panels are one of the post's special architectural features.

When rehabilitation construction began in December 2006, the ceilings were more than a century old and covered by so many layers of paint that they had begun to lose their ornamental detail. Adding insult to injury, the paint was lead-based, which made it a health hazard.

The cleaning and restoration of the pressed-metal panels was a labor-intensive process. The historic architects and their contractors prepared for this project as though they were assembling a giant jigsaw puzzle. The first task was to document and identify the precise location of each individual ceiling panel. Literally every panel from every ceiling in every room in every building was individually numbered so that when the pieces were cleaned and ready for re-installation, they could be put back in the correct spot.

Once the panels were safely removed, they needed to be thoroughly cleaned. Using traditional methods, removing several layers of thick paint can be a messy and toxic job. But through experimentation, project architects discovered that if they froze the metal panels and then flexed them, the paint layers would pop off the stiff metal.

For this process, large wooden boxes full of panels were placed in on-site commercial-size freezers. Once they were sufficiently cold, the individual panels were removed, gently flexed and tapped with brushes. In most cases, the paint flaked right off. Any paint stubbornly remaining was carefully removed with chisels. All the lead paint was appropriately secured and stored in hazardous-material containers for proper disposal.

Once the metal panels were clean, it was easy to see their original decorative designs. As they were carefully replaced, special care was taken to ensure that the original design and directional pattern of each ceiling was recreated. The panels in the residential buildings then had a fresh coat of paint applied and were ready for the next one hundred years.

Visitors may notice that in some areas, the bare metal of the cleaned panels has been left unpainted. The decision was made to leave these ceilings in their unpainted condition in the public spaces to give a more contemporary look. These natural ceilings can be seen in the Farley Bar, Murray Circle restaurant, Mercantile Center and Reception room.

Above: The Frank House was originally the hospital steward's residence. Now the building functions as a guest house with two bedrooms, living room, enclosed sun porch and separate kitchen.

Opposite, above: Murray Circle, the elegant restaurant at Cavallo Point, is located in one of the post's former military barracks. Historic architectural features such as the pressed-metal ceilings and cast iron columns were incorporated into the new decor.

Opposite, below: Cavallo Point's newly constructed Healing Arts Center & Spa.

When Congress created the National Park Service in 1916, it made the new agency responsible for the protection of land set aside to safeguard America's cultural and natural heritage. These areas were to be managed "by such means as will leave them unimpaired for the enjoyment of future generations," a directive that has guided the agency's approach to preservation and conservation for almost a century.

Here at Fort Baker, in the shadow of the Golden Gate, the National Park Service and its partners, including the tenants of Horseshoe Cove, work together to protect its historic buildings, natural resources, spectacular views, endangered species and recreational opportunities.

The National Park Service now oversees more than 300 historic, cultural, natural and recreational areas. According to historian, writer and environmentalist Wallace Stegner, "National parks are the best idea we ever had. Absolutely American, absolutely democratic, they reflect us at our best rather than our worst." Stegner's observation is wonderfully borne out at Fort Baker, where in many ways, swords have truly been beaten into plowshares—beautiful ones, at that.

Acknowledgments

The publisher and authors would like to thank the following individuals for their interest, time and assistance, all of which were generously given during the development of this book: National Park Service subject specialists Steve Haller, Steve Kasierski and Paul Scolari, for reviewing the text; National Park Service interpreters Will Elder and Dan Ng, for their photographs (and Will for his review of the text for the natural history of Horseshoe Cove); Amanda Williford, reference archivist, GGNRA Park Archives and Records Center, for her help with photo research and scanning; Brian Dillon, for use of family photos; Bolling W. Smith, for photo assistance; Rachel Steele of the University of Alaska, Fairbanks, for her help with Louis Choris image research; Nick Tipon, Federated Indians of Graton Rancheria, for his review of "The First Residents" chapter; and Cavallo Point's Leigh Vogen, who observed that the history of this remarkable post should be documented in a book.

Appendix 1
Commanding Officers, Fort Baker, California

Capt. Henry C. Daines, 3rd Artillery: July 7, 1897, to February 5, 1898

Capt. Frank Hess, 3rd Artillery: February 5, 1898, to March 9, 1898

Capt. William E. Birkhimer, 3rd Artillery: March 9, 1898, to June 7, 1898

Capt. Theodore J. Hay, California Volunteer Artillery: June 7, 1898, to September 30, 1898

Capt. Herbert Chcynski, California Volunteer Artillery: September 30, 1898, to ?

2nd Lieut. Henry Butner, 3rd Artillery: January 28, 1899, to August 20, 1899

2nd Lieut. Harry L. James, 3rd Artillery: August 20, 1899, to January 8, 1900

2nd Lieut. Henry B. Clark, 3rd Artillery: January 8, 1900, to July 20, 1900

Capt. R.F. Gardner, 3rd Artillery: July 20, 1900, to ?

2nd Lieut. Guy E. Carleton, 3rd Artillery: ? to November 7, 1901

Capt. H.H. Ludlew, Coast Artillery: November 7, 1901, to July 21, 1902

Lt. Col. Abner C. Merrill, Coast Artillery: July 21, 1902, to May 22, 1903

Capt. Harold E. Cloke, Coast Artillery: May 22, 1903, to June 2, 1903

Capt. E. T. Wilson, Coast Artillery (June 2, 1903, to October 5, 1903)

Lt. Col. Luigi Lamia, Coast Artillery: October 5, 1903, to December 10, 1905

Capt. Henry B. Clark, Coast Artillery: December 10, 1905, to January 13, 1906

Lt. Col. Robert H. Patterson, Coast Artillery: January 13, 1906, to June 9, 1906

Capt. Henry B. Clark, Coast Artillery: June 9, 1906, to October 25, 1906

Lt. Col. Adam Slaker, Coast Artillery: October 25, 1906, to April 26, 1907

Capt. Henry B. Clark, Coast Artillery: April 26, 1907, to May 11, 1907

Lt. Col. Adam Slaker, Coast Artillery: May 11, 1907, to September 29, 1908

Capt. Alden Trotter, Coast Artillery: September 29, 1908, to February 3, 1909

Capt. Raymond H. Fenner, Coast Artillery Corps: February 3, 1909, to February 19, 1909

Major John W. Ruckman, Coast Artillery Corps: February 19, 1909, to June 18, 1909

Capt. Raymond H. Fenner, Coast Artillery Corps: June 18, 1909, to June 28, 1909

Major John W. Ruckman, Coast Artillery Corps: June 18, 1909, to May 13, 1910

Capt. Leonard T. Waldron, Coast Artillery Corps: May 13, 1910, to July 13, 1910

Major John W. Ruckman, Coast Artillery Corps: July 13, 1910, to October 27, 1910

Major Ira A. Haynes, Coast Artillery Corps: October 27, 1910, to March 27, 1911

Capt. Leonard T. Waldron, Coast Artillery Corps: March 27, 1911, to September 7, 1911

Col. John C. W. Brooks, Coast Artillery Corps: September 7, 1911, to February 5, 1912

Major Sam F. Bottoms, Coast Artillery Corps: February 5, 1912, to August 7, 1912

Major Thomas B. Lamoreaux, Coast Artillery Corps: August 7, 1912, to November 6, 1912

Lt. Col. Oscar I. Straub, Coast Artillery Corps: November 6, 1912, to February 15, 1913

Major Thomas B. Lamoreaux, Coast Artillery Corps: February 15, 1913, to September 1, 1914

Major Henry H. Whitney, Coast Artillery Corps: September 1, 1914, to September 19, 1914

Major M. C. Buckey, Coast Artillery Corps: September 19, 1914, to November 18, 1914

Capt. H. C. Merriam, Coast Artillery Corps: November 18, 1914, to January 15, 1915

Major M.C. Buckey, Coast Artillery Corps: January 16, 1915, to Deccmber 18, 1915

Capt. H. C. Merriam, Coast Artillery Corps: December 19, 1915, to February 1, 1916

Major M. C. Buckey, Coast Artillery Corps: February 2, 1916, to November 1, 1916

Capt. Francis M. Hinkle, Coast Artillery Corps: November 2, 1916, to August 31, 1917

Capt. H. W. Stephenson, Coast Artillery Corps: September 1, 1917, to April 23, 1917

Capt. H. E. Whiteside, Coast Artillery: April 24, 1918, to May 31, 1918

Capt. James B. Muir, Coast Artillery: June 1, 1918, to June 4, 1918

Colonel H. G. Mathewson, Coast Artillery: June 5, 1918, to July 8, 1918

Major C. D. Peirce, Coast Artillery: July 9, 1918, to August 16, 1918

Major W. H. Mallett, Coast Artillery: August 17, 1918, to October 19, 1918

1st Lieut. Frederick J. Kelley, Coast Artillery: October 20, 1918, to November 3, 1918

1st Lieut. Albert Olson, Coast Artillery: November 4, 1918, to November 18, 1918

Lt. Col. C. J. Mund, Coast Artillery: November 19, 1918, to June 27, 1919

Col. Charles D. Winn, Coast Artillery: June 28, 1919, to August 23, 1920

Major I. E. Titus, Coast Artillery Corps: August 23, 1920, to December 18, 1922

Major Samuel T. Stewart, Coast Artillery Corps: December 18, 1922, to January 22, 1923

Major O. G. Pitz, Coast Artillery Corps: January 22, 1923, to December 20, 1923

Capt. Manley B. Gibson, Coast Artillery Corps: December 20, 1923, to February 15, 1926

2nd. Lieut. Karl C. Frank, Coast Artillery Corps: February 15, 1926, to April 19, 1926

Capt. Manley B. Gibson, Coast Artillery Corps: April 19, 1926, to October 25, 1926

Major. H. A. Bagg, Coast Artillery Corps: October 25, 1926, to February 23, 1927

Capt. Roy T. Barrett, 6th Coast Artillery: February 23, 1927, to March 1, 1927

Capt. Manley B. Gibson, 6th Coast Artillery: March 1, 1927, to March 2, 1927

Major Reginald B. Cocroft, 6th Coast Artillery: March 2, 1927, to June 30, 1928

Capt. James B. Muir, 6th Coast Artillery: July 1, 1928, to August 6, 1928

Major Joseph D. Brown, 6th Coast Artillery: August 6, 1928, to September 26, 1930

Capt. James B. Muir, Jr., 6th Coast Artillery: September 26, 1930, to February 16, 1931

Major Edward W. Turner, 6th Coast Artillery: February 17, 1931, to October 15, 1932

1st. Lieut. Paul B. Nelson, 6th Coast Artillery: October 15, 1932, to November 15, 1932

Capt. G. F. Ericson, 6th Coast Artillery: November 15, 1932, to May 2, 1933

1st. Lieut. Paul B. Nelson, 6th Coast Artillery: May 2, 1933, to June 5, 1933

1st. Lieut. Norman Simmonds, 6th Coast Artillery: June 5, 1933, to June 19, 1933

Major B. S. Dubois, 6th Coast Artillery: June 19, 1933, to August 7, 1934

Capt. Arnold D. Amoroso, 6th Coast Artillery: August 7, 1934, to December 3, 1934

1st. Lieut. George F. Heaney, Jr., 6th Coast Artillery: December 3, 1934, to January 1, 1935

Major G. H. Ericson, 6th Coast Artillery: January 1, 1935, to June 25, 1935

Capt. H. G. Archibald, 6th Coast Artillery: June 26, 1935, to August 24, 1935

Capt. Dean Luce, 6th Coast Artillery: August 25, 1935, to October 14, 1935

Capt. Rodney C. Jones, 6th Coast Artillery: October 15, 1935, to January 21, 1936

Major E. B. McCarthy, 6th Coast Artillery: January 22, 1936, to March 6, 1937

Major W. W. Irvine, 6th Coast Artillery: March 7, 1937, to May 16, 1937

Major Manley B. Gibson, 6th Coast Artillery: May 16, 1937, to July 9, 1939

Major E. R. Crowell, 6th Coast Artillery: July 19, 1939, to July 14, 1939

Major Marvin J. McKinney, 6th Coast Artillery: July 15, 1939, to August 18, 1939

Lt. Col. E. R. Crowell, 6th Coast Artillery: August 19, 1939, to January 24, 1941

Major John H. Fonvielle, 6th Coast Artillery: January 25, 1941, to August 30, 1943

Lt. Col. John Schonher, 6th Coast Artillery: August 31, 1943, to December 1, 1943

Col. J. C. Hutson, 6th Coast Artillery: December 2, 1943, to January 23, 1944

Lt. Col. Sheldon H. Smith, 6th Coast Artillery: January 24, 1944, to January 24, 1944

Col. Kenneth Rowntree, 6th Coast Artillery: January 25, 1944, to May 3, 1944

Lt. Col. John Schonher, 6th Coast Artillery: May 4, 1944, to October 17, 1944

Lt. Col. John Schonher, 173rd Coast Artillery Bn (HD)*: October 18, 1944, to August 15, 1945

Capt. George M. Lieber, 173rd Coast Artillery Bn (HD)*: August 16, 1945, to August 31, 1945

Lt. Col. John Schonher, 173rd Coast Artillery Bn (HD)*: September 1, 1945, to June 16, 1946

Lt. Col. Sheldon H. Smith, Coast Artillery Corps: June 16, 1946, to June 30, 1946

Lt. Col. E. Carl. Englehart, Coast Artillery Corps: July 1, 1946, to March 11, 1948

Col. E. Carl. Englehart, Coast Artillery Corps: March 12, 1948, to January 13, 1949

Lt. Col. H. A. MccLean, Coast Artillery Corps: January 14, 1949, to December 27, 1949

Lt. Col. M. M. Santos, Coast Artillery Corps: December 28, 1949, to ?

* In October 1944, the Coast Artillery Corps was reorganized and the old 6th Coast Artillery became the 173rd Coast Artillery Battalion (Harbor Defense)

Appendix 2
A Partial List of US Army Units Assigned to Fort Baker, California

Battery C, 3rd US Artillery

Battery D, 3rd US Artillery

Battery E, 3rd US. Artillery

Battery I, 3rd US Artillery

Battery L, 3rd US Artillery

Battery O, 3rd US Artillery

1st Battalion, Heavy Artillery, California US Volunteers

Convalescent Company Number 3

32nd Company, Coast Artillery

61st Company, Coast Artillery

67th Company, Coast Artillery

68th Company, Coast Artillery

148th Company, Coast Artillery

161st Company, Coast Artillery

Companies B, D, F, I, & M, 5th Regiment, National Guard of California

1st Company, Coast Artillery Corps, Fort Baker

2nd Company, Coast Artillery Corps, Fort Baker

3rd Company, Coast Artillery Corps, Fort Baker

11th Company, Coast Artillery Corps, San Francisco

12th Company, Coast Artillery Corps, San Francisco

13th Company, Coast Artillery Corps, San Francisco

17th Company, Coast Artillery Corps, San Francisco

45th Company, Coast Artillery Corps, San Francisco

24th Balloon Company

Battery F, 6th Coast Artillery

Battery G, 6th Coast Artillery

Battery K, 6th Coast Artillery

Battery A, 6th Coast Artillery Battalion (Harbor Defense)

Battery M, 6th Coast Artillery Battalion (Harbor Defense)

Battery A, 67th Coast Artillery Battalion (Harbor Defense)

Battery A, 130th Coast Artillery Battalion (Anti-Aircraft)

Headquarters & Headquarters Battery, 173rd Coast Artillery Battalion (Harbor Defense)

Battery A, 174th Coast Artillery Battalion (Harbor Defense)

Battery B, 174th Coast Artillery Battalion (Harbor Defense)

4th, 11th, 21st, and 29th CAMP Stations

Battery E, Harbor Defenses of San Francisco (aka HDSF)

Battery F, Harbor Defenses of San Francisco (aka HDSF)

Battery G, Harbor Defenses of San Francisco (aka HDSF)

4th Mine Planter Battery

11th Mine Planter Battery

21st Mine Planter Battery

Mine Detachment, Seacoast Branch of the Artillery School

Artillery Detachment, Seacoast Branch of the Artillery School

Seacoast Service Test Section

29th CAMP (Maybach)

Headquarters & Headquarters Detachment, 2nd Battalion, Coast Artillery

2nd Coast Artillery Battery (Mines)

36th Coast Artillery Battery, 61st Coast Artillery Battalion

13th Signal Operating Company

Troop Headquarters Section, Headquarters Detachment, SBTAS

6th Army Medical Laboratory

561st Port Construction Engineer Corps

6th Army Marine Boat Repair Facility

47th Anti-aircraft Artillery (AAA) Brigade

6th Region, Army Air Defense Command (ARADCOM)

91st Division (Training Support)

Appendix 3
Permanent Fortifications and Armament, Fort Baker

1870S ERA

Name	Armament	Armed	Disarmed	Notes
Cavallo Battery	Planned for: 1 x 15 inch Rodman guns on front pintle carriages 1 x 20 inch Rodman gun on a center pintle carriage 6 x 13 inch mortars	1898 (3 x 8 inch rifled Rodmans on front pintle iron carriages	c. 1909	Armed as part of Spanish-American War emergency defenses. Magazines later used as TNT storage for minefields
Cavallo Point Battery	Planned for: 2 x 15 inch Rodman guns on front pintle carriages	n/a	n/a	Demolished during construction of Battery Yates
Cliff Battery	Planned for: 5 x 15 inch Rodman guns on front pintle carriages	n/a	n/a	Demolished during construction of Battery Spencer
Gravelly Beach Battery	Planned for: 12 x 15 inch Rodman guns on front pintle carriages	1873 (1 gun)	c. 1899	Gun installed for test purposes. Partially demolished during construction of Battery Kirby
Ridge Battery	Planned for: 4 x 15 inch Rodman guns on front pintle carriages 4 x 13 inch mortars	1893 (4 guns)	c. 1909	Guns transferred from old West Battery, Presidio of San Francisco

ENDICOTT ERA, LIME POINT AREA (1893-1905)

Name	Armament	Armed	Disarmed	Notes
Battery Duncan	2 x 8 inch rifles M1888 on barbette carriages M1892	1899	1918	Battery's magazines later used for TNT storage for minefields
Battery Kirby	2 x 12 inch rifles M1895 on disappearing carriages M1897	1900	1937 (gun 1)	1941 (gun 2)
Battery Spencer	3 x 12 inch rifles M1888 on barbette carriages M1892	1897	1917 (gun 3) 1943 (guns 1 & 2)	Gun #3 sent to Fort Miley, San Francisco
Battery Wagner	2 x 5 inch rifles M1896 on balanced pillar mounts M1896	1901	1917	Gun installed for test purposes. Partially demolished during construction of Battery Kirby
Battery Yates	6 x 3 inch rapid-fire rifles M1902M1 on pedestal mounts M1902	1905	1940 (guns 1 & 2); 1942 (guns 3 & 4); 1946 (guns 5 & 6)	Guns 1 & 2 sent to Fort Cronkhite Guns 3 & 4 sent to Fort Point

ENDICOTT ERA, POINT BONITA AREA (LATER FORT BARRY) (1901-1907)

Name	Armament	Armed	Disarmed	Notes
Battery Alexander	8 x 12 inch rifled mortars M1890M1 on mortar carriages M1896M1	1905	1918 1943	4 mortars removed 1918 for WWI use overseas 4 mortars scrapped during WWII
Battery Mendell	2 x 12 inch rifles M1895 on disappearing carriages M1897	1905	1943	
Battery O'Rorke	4 x 3 inch rapid fire rifles M1903 on pedestal mounts M1903	1905	1946	
Battery Rathbone	4 x 6 inch rapid-fire rifles M1900 on barbette carriages M1900	1905	1946	Subdivided in 1922 into two batteries: Rathbone and McIndoe
Battery Guthrie	4 x 6 inch rapid fire rifles M1900 on barbette carriages M1900	1905	1946	Subdivided in 1922 into two batteries: Guthrie and Smith

Name	Armament	Armed	Disarmed	Notes
Gravelly Beach 3 inch AMTB battery	2 x 3 inch rapid fire rifles M1902 on pedestal mounts M1902	1942	1943	Guns transferred from Fort Cronkhite; sent to Fort Point. Presidio of San Francisco
Gravelly Beach 90 mm AMTB battery	2 x 90 mm M1 rapid-fire dual purpose guns on Fixed M3 shield mounts 2 x 90 mm M1 rapid fire dual purpose guns on Mobile M1 mounts	1942	1946	

Photograph and Illustration Credits

Ray Aker: p. 4 (top)

Brian B. Chin: p. 58 (bottom)

Brian D. Dillon Collection: p. 34 (lower left): p. 53

Golden Gate Bridge, Highway and Transportation District: p. 53

Golden Gate NRA/Park Archives and Records Center: Title page (PAM Prints Coll., GOGA-1766); iv (TASC Negative Collection, GOGA 35301.0237); 16 (Interp. Negative Coll., GOGA-2316, 77-C-292); 18, upper left (TASC Negative Coll., GOGA 35301.2000); 19 (Interp. Negative Coll., GOGA-2316, 77-C-290); 21 (Fort Point Photograph Coll.); 22, upper left (GOGA 17985.01); 22, lower left (PAM Prints Coll., GOGA-1766); 24, upper left (Interp. Negative Coll., GOGA-2316); 25, upper right (TASC Negative Coll., GOGA 35301.1997); 25, lower right (PAM Prints Coll., GOGA-1766); 26 (PAM Prints Coll., GOGA-1766); 27, lower right (Interp. Negative Coll., GOGA-2316, 80-C-128); 28 (Army Drawing Coll., Drawer 195, Folder 1); 29 (PAM Prints Coll., GOGA-1766); 30 (TASC Negative Coll., GOGA 35301.0912); 31 (GOGA 32456); 32, upper right (Donald Thomas Coll., GOGA-2605); 33, top (TASC Negative Coll., GOGA 35301.0907); 33, lower right (Fort Baker Postcards Coll., GOGA 19193.002); 35, upper left (PAM Prints Coll., GOGA-1766); 35, upper right (Donald Thomas Coll., GOGA-2605-005); 35, lower right (PAM Prints Coll., GOGA-1766); 39 (Fort Baker Aerial Photos Coll., GOGA 34287); 43 (PAM Prints Coll., GOGA-1766); 42, lower left (Fort Baker Historical Record of Buildings, GOGA 32426); 44, lower left (Edwin Long Family Album, GOGA-3411.022); 46, lower left (Fort Baker ROTC Photograph Coll., GOGA 40096); 45, upper right (Fort Baker Building Book, GOGA 32426); 47, lower right (William P. Banta Letterman Album, GOGA 35249); 49, lower right (Elanora Hoop Collection, GOGA .024); 50, lower left (Edwin Long Family Album, GOGA-3411.056); 50, lower right (Edwin Long Family Album, GOGA-3411.058); 54, top (King Corona Fort Barry Photograph Coll., GOGA 2039.003); 54, upper right (PAM Prints Coll.; GOGA-1766); 61, upper right (Sheldon Smith Coast Artillery Coll., GOGA-3059); 62 and 63, top (Corps of Engineers Photographs Coll., GOGA-18017); 64, upper left (TASC Negative Coll., GOGA 35301.0905); 64, upper right (PAM Prints Coll., GOGA-1766); 65 (Corps of Engineers Photographs Coll., GOGA-18017); 66, top (Donald Thomas Coll., GOGA-3311.005); 69 (TASC Negative Coll., GOGA 35301.2021); 70 (TASC Negative Coll., GOGA 35301); 71 (TASC Negative Coll., GOGA 35301.0903); 72 (TASC Negative Coll., GOGA 35301); 73, top (Schaefer Family NIKE Photo Coll., GOGA 18513.003); 74–75, all (PAM Prints Coll., GOGA-1766); 76 (TASC Negative Coll., GOGA 35301.0920); 83, upper left (Fort Baker Historical Record of Buildings, GOGA 32426)

Kodiak Greenwood: pp. 81, 86; 87 (lower right)

Library of Congress: pp. 38 (upper left); 38 (upper right); p. 42; 55 (center right); 55 (lower right); 59

John A. Martini Collection: pp. 24 (lower left); 27 (upper left); 32 (left); 34 (upper left); 58 (upper left); 66 (bottom); 67; 78; 82

Rob McCall: p. 59 (upper right)

Gordon Miller: p. 5

National Archives & Records Administration: pp. 16 (lower left); 18 (lower right); 19

National Park Service: pp. 44 (lower right); 77 (top); 77 (bottom); 83 (upper right); 83 (lower right); 84 (all); 85

Lawrence Ormsby: endpapers; pp. 12; 13; 14; 15; 40; 41; 44 (top); 45 (top); 46 (top); 48 (top); 50 (top); 51 (top)

Puget Sound Coast Artillery Museum: p. 54 (lower right)

David Rumsey Map Collection, Cartography Associates: p. 8

San Francisco Maritime National Historical Park: pp. 4 (Ray Aker illustration); 10–11 (SAFR A11.4,528)

San Francisco Public Library: p. 63, lower right (CA. Fort Baker, negative #6649)

Sausalito Historical Society: p. 37 (Accession 2002-10)

B.W. Smith Collection: pp. 55 (upper right);59 (bottom); 60 (upper right)

Sam Stokes Collection: p. 61 (lower left)

U.S. Army Signal Corps: pp. 52; 56; 60 (lower left)

University of Alaska, Fairbanks: p. 2 ("Voyage pittoresque autour du monde," Alaska and Polar Regions Collections, Plate XII, B0083)

University of California, Berkeley, Bancroft Library: p. 9 (Frank B. Rodolph Photograph Coll., BANC PIC 1905.17147:99-PIC)

David Wakely: p. 87 (upper right)

Index

*Numbers in **bold** type refer to illustrations.*

This book was designed and typeset in Trump Mediaeval and Impact by Carole Thickstun, Ormsby & Thickstun Interpretive Design. It was printed on a Manroland press using soy-based inks on 80 pound Garda Text, Matte White (interior) and 15 point Carolina (cover) by Friesens Printing, Canada.